Introd

A lot of regular walkers dismiss
satisfying walking, but in ignorii
that can provide excellent outd
suit those who like long walks as well as t ….er ones. It is
hoped that this book will encourage you tc …p your boots and give this
pleasant area a go. It is principally concerned with the great Sandstone Ridge
which runs down the west side of Cheshire from the coastal regions around
Frodsham before terminating towards the Shropshire border some thirty
miles distant. Along and around this elevated ground you will find sandstone
outcrops, lovely woodland, ancient castles, meres and many lovely villages,
as well as the impressive City of Chester.

All these walks are either on the hill country of the ridge or very close to
it. The walking climbs to all the tops that can be reached and explores the
foothills that blend into the Welsh borderland at the ridge's end. It also takes
in excursions to an ancient mere and explores the great Forest of Delamere,
as well as the rolling heathland of Little Budworth Common. It includes
many of the 'classic' routes in the area but it is difficult to be selective with
such excellent walking on offer. Expect up-and-down paths on the ridge and
rolling fields on the lower ground.

Cheshire is not known for an adverse climate and the ridge never makes
it to the thousand foot mark at any point and is easy to escape from, so you
should never get into trouble with the weather. However, please take the
usual precautions when venturing into hill country – let someone know
where you are going and when you will be back and get an up-to-date forecast
for the weather (09068 500416, then 1601 when asked). Appropriate clothing
should always be worn and a good pair of boots will make some of the
rougher ground easier to walk over.

All of these routes are on rights of way or over access land, and Chester
and Forest of Delamere have good visitor and information centres. The
Sandstone Trail follows the Sandstone Ridge from Frodsham to Whitchurch,
over the border in Shropshire, and many of these routes use parts of it.

Walk 20 takes on the challenge of The Baker Way, linking Chester to the
Delamere Forest. At 13 miles it is the longest and probably most demanding
walk in this book.

You'll enjoy walking in this area and if you choose your days carefully to
get the best weather you will find a region you will return to often on your
outings.

Enjoy your walking!

FRODSHAM HILL & BEACON

DESCRIPTION This is a real roller-coaster ridge and hill walk on the very last of the high ground at the northern end of the Cheshire sandstone ridge. The wooded heights of Woodhouse Hill and Overton Hill have long been lumped together by locals under the collective name of Frodsham Hill, and the outcrop and war memorial beacon are a landmark for miles around. This charming and energetic route starts from a high-level car park and works a circuit around the higher ground of the hill for about 5 miles. A lovely ridge path along the sandstone edges is followed by an exploration of the network of footpaths that criss-cross the upper reaches of the hill, and a return is made along a hidden clough (ravine) and finishes with a promenade along a further section of high ridge following the later stages of The Sandstone Trail. Allow 3 hours.

START From the Cheshire County Council car park for the Sandstone Trail at Beacon Hill above Frodsham. SJ 518766.

DIRECTIONS The car park is best reached by using a combination of the M56 (either junction 14 or 12) and the A56 Frodsham/Helsby road. The car park is located south of the town of Frodsham and above it on the upper reaches of Beacon Hill (the one with the communications masts on) which is best found by following the B5152 south from Frodsham and on the outskirts, in the region of Overton, following signs for the Forest Hills Hotel.

BACKGROUND INFORMATION
See page 4

I Exit the car park onto the road and go RIGHT along the The Sandstone Trail for a short distance to go LEFT down a sunken green lane (still on the Sandstone Trail). Cross a stile to the left of a gate to go straight over a golf course, taking care and following the markers and the faint path. Near the end of the crossing, the path dips downhill slightly and continues to reach trees and a path junction by a sign. Go RIGHT signposted for 'Frodsham Centre and Sandstone Trail'.

Head along the ridge edge, climbing uphill to pass a bench and a viewpoint and continue on the edge of the escarpment, curving left at a marker post, and begin to descend to enter Frodsham Hill Wood. Follow the winding edge path below sandstone outcrops. At a crossing of paths go RIGHT up steps and curve left at the top heading towards the Forest Hills Hotel. Stay LEFT at a set of steps keeping on the ridge path until you pick up the Sandstone Trail again at a path junction a little further on. Continue on to reach the War Memorial obelisk and viewpoint. Pass behind it to curve left after benches, picking up a good track to descend on steps into trees. Go RIGHT at a T-junction following The Sandstone Trail. When a junction of paths is reached with 'Frodsham Centre' indicated, continue AHEAD to curve through woods and exit onto a lane at the Belle Monte Hotel.

2 Walk past the hotel to reach a lane and go RIGHT uphill for a short distance to take a footpath LEFT along the middle slopes of Beacon Hill. Stay on this track through trees to reach more open ground and eventually cross an access track continuing on the other side through a gate to head slightly downhill on a grassy track. Join a drive by a lamp-post and walk down it to reach a road via a squeeze stile or a gate. Go LEFT down the road for a hundred metres or so and take the footpath RIGHT to enter the golf course via a hedge gap and walk along the right-hand side of it towards trees ahead. Exit the golf course in the right-hand corner to take a good track with a hedge right and a fence left. Rise towards the woods ignoring any turnings off the track and drop down to cross a farm access track, and go through a kissing gate on the opposite side to enter a field. Cross this field in the direction of a house ahead, using the path, and exit onto a lane via a kissing gate.

3 Turn RIGHT along the lane (it can be busy at times so take care) to reach a point just before the road junction left and Riley Bank Farm ahead left. Here go RIGHT through a kissing gate by the road sign to go down the right side of the field by a fence on the right to pick up a good path that descends steeply into a deep hollow and passes through a kissing gate to continue along the floor of the hollow. Go LEFT at a path junction. Follow the path along the hollow which widens out further along. Cross a stile along the way, and as houses appear up on the left exit the track via a kissing gate going RIGHT up a muddy lane for a short distance to turn LEFT as the field opens out and follow the bottom left edge of the field to reach a kissing gate on the edge of woodland. Pass through this to re-join the Sandstone Trail at a T-junction.

4 Go RIGHT on The Sandstone Trail heading uphill on a wide track. Ignore a turning left for Woodhouse Hill and continue to climb on a sunken track amongst trees to reach more open ground, and climb up large steps to reach a T-junction of paths going left, still following The Sandstone Trail. Keep ahead and, when the track splits, stay left near an old wall on the right still following The Sandstone Trail and curving slightly right to reach the edge of the ridge. Drop sharply down the other side on the path to reach a bench and viewpoint and go RIGHT along the edge of the ridge following the good path back towards Frodsham Hill. Stay on the good path (The Sandstone Trail) to pick up the golf course edge again and finally descend on steps to cross a wide hollow via a bridge and continue on a good track beneath sandstone outcrops. At a path junction beneath sandstone cliffs go RIGHT following The Sandstone Trail for 'Frodsham', climbing up a hollow and turning back LEFT up steep steps. At the top continue on the path to climb RIGHT up a few more steps and reach the path junction at the edge of the golf course from your outward journey.

5 Go RIGHT for the 'Sandstone Trail Beacon Hill car park' and walk back carefully over the golf course to cross a stile, climb up the green track and go RIGHT along the lane, then LEFT back into the car park.

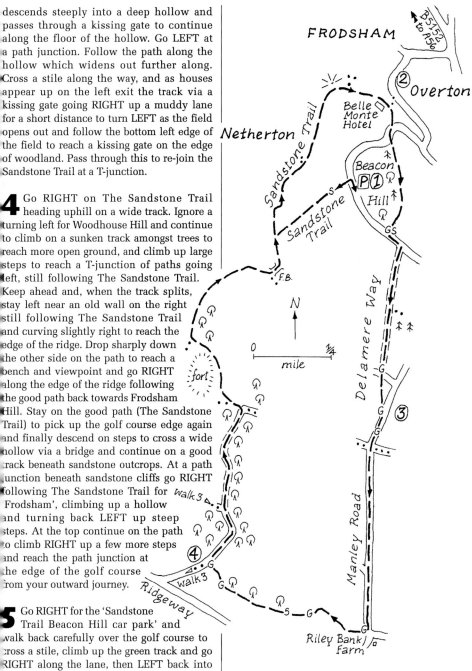

FRODSHAM

Overton

Netherton

Belle Monte Hotel

Beacon

Hill

Sandstone Trail

Delamere Way

N

fort

F.B.

Walk 3

Ridgeway

walk 3

Manley Road

Riley Bank Farm

0   ¼
mile

BACKGROUND INFORMATION

WALK 1
FRODSHAM HILL

Frodsham Hill is, in reality, a combination of Woodhouse Hill, Foxhill and Overton Hill and used to be the site of a small fair with a lovely helter-skelter, popular with local families on summer days many years ago. Now an excellent hotel sits on the escarpment, and a nearby war memorial is visible for many miles around. The area is very popular with walkers. The Sandstone Trail finally ends here after its long journey from near Whitchurch. The views across the Mersey estuary almost four hundred feet below the ridge are stunning. The flat marshlands make an open vista and Liverpool is clearly seen on fine days.

The Sandstone Trail, which a lot of the walks in this book use, is 34 miles long and runs from Grindley Brook near Whitchurch, just over the border in Shropshire, to finish at Frodsham near the hill. Most people walk it over two days but it can be done in one day of good weather in the summer. It keeps to the high ground of the Cheshire sandstone ridge as much as it can, and passes through the great Forest of Delamere.

WALK 3
WOODHOUSE HILL & HILLFORTS

The sandstone ridge that runs along the hillside above Frodsham is known locally as Frodsham Hill, but it is in reality a collection of the summits of Overton Hill, Woodhouse Hill and a little bit of Fox Hill all grouped together. In true hill terms there is probably only really one top, but the ridge certainly drops near the middle to give two separate summits. It can all be a little confusing but don't worry – this is not a summit-bagging region but a place to come and enjoy the magnificent walking country and the great views.

Many Cheshire tops were the sites of hill forts around 2000 years ago. Woodhouse Hill had one on it, and when it was occupied it would have been surrounded by deep defensive ditches and high ramparts, some of which can still be traced it you know what to look for. The fort would have

contained a small village of wooden huts. It was a great defensive and look out point for the flat surrounding marshland by the Mersey Estuary.

The Longster Trail is a 10 mile route from Helsby Hill to Chester.

WALK 4
THE NEW PALE AREA

The New Pale is an area on the fringes of the vast forest of Delamere and is relatively unknown by many walkers who visit the area. A lot of the region's long distance tracks meander around here but most walkers stay with in the forest boundaries and in doing so miss a lovely area of rolling upland which offers great views in all directions, from the Clwydian Hills of North Wales to the Great Sandstone Ridge of Cheshire towards Beeston, and even views over the Pennine hills of Lancashire. This is superb walking country with lots of ups and downs.

The New Pale was originally a hunting area and forest enclosure before it was cleared. Here deer would have been hunted regularly four to five hundred years ago. The whole are would have been a Royal Hunting Forest at that time and became known as 'The Forest of the Meres and Pools' or 'Forest de la Mere' by regular visitors. Both Oliver Cromwell and the Methodist preacher John Wesley are rumoured to have stayed at the New Pale Lodge (passed on this route), but there is no firm evidence to support this.

The Eddisbury Way, which is followed on this route, is a 16 mile walk linking Frodsham to the Sandstone Trail at Burwardsley, following rights of way and lovely quiet lanes.

WALK 5
HATCHMERE & FLAXMERE

Hatchmere Lake has long been one of the popular picnic spots in Delamere Forest and has a large car park with toilets (seasonal) facing it. It is a typical Cheshire Mere (with a nice pub next to it to boot) and is very popular with fishermen, being the haunt of large pike. Numerous birds are attracted here all year round. The mere is glacial in origin and is believed to have been formed by a huge piece of ice that was left behind at the end of the last ice age. Please stay off the landing stages as they are private.

Flaxmere once shared Hatchmere's attributes but was shallower, and being situated in more enclosed ground, it slowly filled with sediment until it became dry. The area you see nowadays is rough heathland and is the haunt of numerous insects, birds and animals, but it has not settled enough yet to allow farming.

Parts of both The Delamere Loop and The Delamere Way are used on this route. The Delamere Loop is a 22 mile circuit of bridleways for walkers and horse riders, but is also popular in sections with mountain bikers.

The Delamare Way is a 21 mile walk that goes from Frodsham to Warrington passing through Delamere Forest en route.

WALK 6
DELAMERE FOREST

Situated about ten miles from Chester and close to the M56 motorway, Delamere Forest is a mix of deciduous and coniferous trees covering 2,300 acres, and is the largest area of woodland in Cheshire. Its 'Go Ape' facility is the biggest in the UK and in the summer regular music concerts are held in the Forest. It is managed by The Forestry Commission and, because of its central location, is an extremely popular weekend venue for walkers and cyclists.

Almost a thousand years ago the Normans created the first woodland here to give them hunting grounds, and the well-managed forest you walk through today is all that remains of their two hunting forests of Mondrem and Mara.

The monument
on Frodsham Hill.
Walk 1.

WALK 2

HELSBY HILL

DESCRIPTION Helsby Hill brings the great Sandstone Ridge of West Cheshire to an abrupt halt in a dramatic cliff of sheer sandstone which gives an imposing backdrop to the bustling town of Helsby far below it. Helsby Hill is a great viewpoint and justifiably popular with walkers and locals alike, many of whom use its open spaces to exercise their dogs. This short route of 3 miles visits the unusual green trig point on the summit twice as it winds a way around the hillside and the lanes and paths to the south. Allow 2 hours.

START From Helsby Hill Quarry Woodland car park (free) near Helsby. SJ 491749.

DIRECTIONS The car park is best reached by using a combination of the M56 (either junction 14 or 12) and the A56 Frodsham/Helsby road and is located close to Helsby on the B5393 Mouldsworth to Helsby road.

I Exit the car park onto the road and go LEFT along it for a short distance to go RIGHT up Hill Road South following signs for 'Helsby Hill'. Climb steeply up the lane to go to the RIGHT of a gate, pass in front of a house and pass through a squeeze stile as the lane ends, to enter National Trust land on Helsby Hill. Follow the track through the woods climbing steadily to reach a path junction and a finger post. Stay LEFT, signposted 'Helsby Hill Top', and climb on a sandstone path to join a wire fence. Follow this up by the edge of the escarpment through the trees, *taking note of the warning sign for the cliffs and keeping any children in the party close to you.* When the fence and trees end, continue along the summit ridge to reach the green trig point.

2 From the trig point head east towards a yellow arrow and a fence keeping the cliffs to the left and re-entering trees to descend curving steeply left and picking up a good path that meanders downwards through the trees with glimpses of fine views. After a level section, descend again with Helsby below left and when the track splits, stay RIGHT on the narrower path to contour

the hillside curving right and descending to reach a track with a stile and footpath sign (Hill Top) on the edge of the woods. Go RIGHT as directed by the signpost for 'Hill Road North ½ Mile'. Pass to the right of a gate and go along a track to descend slightly to a wider track and continue on to join a surfaced lane at a house. Pass the house and walk to the lane end to reach a 'T' junction.

3 Turn LEFT downhill along Hill Road North and walk to the end of it to go RIGHT on another road. Walk along this and when it bends left take the public footpath on the RIGHT over the stile between two gates (signposted 'Helsby Hill'). Go half-LEFT to climb up the meadow, and cross a second stile continuing straight ahead up the next field to a junction of paths with a signpost for The Longster Trail.

4 Pass through the hedge to go RIGHT along the track back towards Helsby Hill. Rise to a kissing gate, passing through to go RIGHT along the field edge, and curve left around the field to pass through another kissing gate on the right to continue on a track and curve right to another kissing gate. Pass through and walk along a green track to exit onto a lane via a metal gate. Go LEFT up the lane to walk to the top passing a parking area and picnic spot on the way.

5 At the top of the lane go LEFT by the cream-coloured house, going left of a gate signposted 'Helsby Hill Top and Helsby Quarry'. Pass to the left of the lake on a good track and walk along it to go RIGHT on a concessionary path just before the woods ahead – this is signposted 'Hill Top'. Follow this path to reach the green trig point on the summit of Helsby Hill for the second time. Go LEFT from the trig and follow your outbound route back down to the finger post and path junction. Here go RIGHT on a narrower path, descending to go LEFT on a path following the edge of the escarpment in the trees. Follow this to curve left back to a squeeze stile near the house at the head of Hill Lane South. Go RIGHT through it and descend the lane. Go RIGHT at the bottom and follow the road for a short distance to go LEFT along an obvious track (signposted

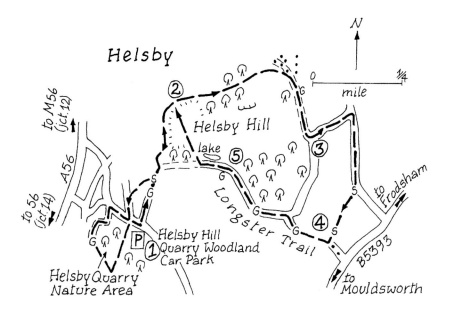

Helsby

Helsby Hill

Robin Hood Lane') as the road the bends right. Descend this enclosed track to reach a cobbled lane by a footpath sign. Go LEFT up lane this staying on it to bend right and keep going until just before a road is reached at a footpath sign. Go sharp LEFT past a bin to walk up a driveway and pass through gates to enter Helsby Quarry Nature Area. Go to the RIGHT of a gate and walk between sandstone outcrops. When the track bends right towards a gate and footpath sign, go LEFT up steps to go to the right of a quarry and follow the path around to the left. Go RIGHT when the path splits, exiting the woods and curving to the right to go LEFT in front of a quarry face on a good track, which you follow uphill, staying on it until you pass a flagpole and go LEFT up steps, passing picnic benches to return to the car park.

HELSBY HILL

Although only 462ft above sea level, it feels much higher when you stand on the breezy summit of Helsby Hill, with the flatlands leading across the Mersey Estuary and the Wirral Peninsula laid out below you. On clear days both of Liverpool's Cathedrals are visible. About two thousand years ago there was once an Iron Age Hillfort on the top, and traces of its earthworks can still be seen.

More recently, the steep sandstone cliffs above Helsby Town have been 'discovered' as a rock-climbing ground and remain popular to this day. Tough routes of between 20 and 90 feet in exposed situations test local climbers on most warm afternoons, when the rocks catch the sun.

WALK 3

WOODHOUSE HILL & FOXHILL WOODS

DESCRIPTION At 3½ miles this is a great little route combining an exploration of the lesser known end of the Frodsham Hill sandstone ridge and the enchanting Foxhill Woods. The area around the summit of Woodhouse Hill (often referred to as Fox Hill) is a maze of paths, but the route described below gives a good chance to explore it. A return is made using a roller coaster section of the Sandstone Trail and a section of the Longster Trail with a little lane walking. 2 hours should be enough for most people to complete this route but why not take longer, as the views are lovely.

START From the Arboretum car park (free) under Foxhill Woods south of Helsby and Frodsham. SJ 505754. There is alternative roadside parking just around the bend on the road once the car park entrance is passed.

DIRECTIONS The car park is best reached by using a combination of the M56 (either junction 14 or 12) and the A56 Frodsham/Helsby road, and is located south of the A56 on the B5393 that leaves the A56 Chester Road between Frodsham and Helsby. The car park is up an access track, off Tarvin Road just before a sharp right bend and a junction going left.

BACKGROUND INFORMATION
See page 4

I Exit the car park, going back down the access track and then LEFT along the road (carefully). Curve right around the bend ignoring the turning left and taking a footpath on the RIGHT by a gate to walk down the right-hand edge of the long field with a brook on the right. Near the field bottom watch for a path to the right into trees and take it to cross the brook on a bridge, continuing on the green lane beyond to reach houses. After a line of white cottages reach a T-junction and go RIGHT up Chestnut Lane passing 'The Nook' to walk to the top of the lane and reach a road.

2 Go LEFT in front of an electrical workshop and walk a short distance to cross carefully near a post box and take the right of way on the RIGHT, up the driveway. As the steep lane reaches a right-hand bend near a house go ahead through a kissing gate to enter the trees of Woodhouse Hill. Go straight on at path junction after a gate to climb steeply up through the woods, curving slightly left and continuing to climb through small sandstone outcrops. Rise up to a fence corner and path junction in a clearer area near a kissing gate and 'Woodhouse Hill' sign.

3 Leave the main path and go RIGHT through the kissing gate, heading into open ground and following the path downhill to reach another kissing gate. Pass through, continuing ahead to rise slightly through a new plantation and curve right uphill on a good path, carrying on to pass through a wall gap. Stay on the path and at the end of the next young plantation on the right, leave the main path turning RIGHT to climb to the pole on the hilltop. Retrace your steps back from here keeping gorse bushes to the right and heading downhill on faint path half-RIGHT to pass to the right-hand side of a bench descending a steep grass slope to pick up a path below it. Go LEFT on this, curving left through a young plantation and under the upper slopes of the hill. Reach a better path at a T-junction in more open ground and go RIGHT, steeply down the slope towards the wooded valley ahead. Pick up an even better path at another junction and go RIGHT down a shallow valley between trees, to curveleft and descend to join a gravel track and drop to a gate and a kissing gate. Pass this to reach a good track in the forest – The Sandstone Trail. Go RIGHT to follow this downhill staying ahead at a path junction to pass a pond. Continue to pass a caravan site and stay on this track (The Sandstone Trail) to reach a road.

4 Go LEFT following The Sandstone Trail uphill on lane, then right, still on the trail opposite the entrance to the caravan site signposted 'Delamere Forest. Enter Ridgeway Wood to take either of the two paths ahead which both converge in a short while and drop down through the woods on steps. Curve left at the bottom following the edge of the woods with a stream to the right to pass a bench and marker post. Cross a bridge over the stream exiting into a field. Stay left by the edge of the woods and follow the field around to curve left and pass through a kissing gate near a wood corner. Follow the Sandstone Trail uphill to pass through a kissing gate and join a lane. Go RIGHT following the lane to pass a junction on the left and carry on until just before Commonside Farm.

5 Here take the public footpath RIGHT (The Longster Trail) through a kissing gate to head down the field, going to the left of the wooded clough ahead and passing to the left of old stile to stay RIGHT when the path splits. Head into the hollow. *NOTE THE NEXT SECTION IS A MAZE OF PATHS SO FOLLOW THE DIRECTIONS CAREFULLY!* Stay RIGHT when the path splits again, keeping on a narrower track by trees to pass through a kissing gate and descend steps. Go right along the field edge, curving left before the stream is reached to head towards a white house and a bridge on very rough ground. Go RIGHT over the bridge climbing steps to the right of the house to cross a stile by a gate and reach a lane. Here go LEFT down Burrows Lane, curving right a little further on, to pass a kissing gate on your left. Continue ahead to reach a road junction. Go LEFT along 'The Ridgeway' continuing along it to the end and join your outward route at a road corner. Go RIGHT and then RIGHT again to walk back up the access track to your car.

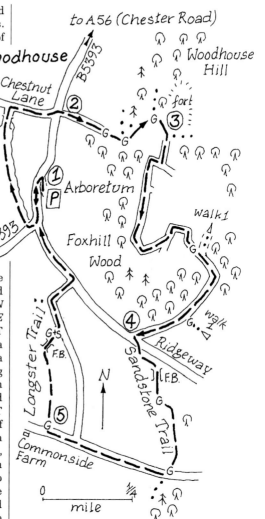

EXPLORING THE NEW PALE AREA

DESCRIPTION The area to the north and west of the wonderful Delamere Forest is criss-crossed with long distance footpaths which converge in the region. They make for great walking, and linking them up makes a superb way to explore the lesser known north-western fringes of the forest as well as the ancient forest enclosure (now mostly open ground) of the upland region called the New Pale. The route is 5¼ miles long and takes a long circular course out of the main forest area using The Sandstone Trail. After walking over and around the New Pale a return is made via good paths through woodland and over fields, with extensive views north over Cheshire, the Wirral and Lancashire, to finally re-enter Delamere Forest, using one of the many paths to return to the car park. This energetic walk involves a fair bit of up and down but is highly enjoyable. It will take about 3½ hours.

START There is an excellent free car park at Barns Bridge Gate on the minor road that runs between Hatchmere and Mouldsworth. It is actually on the Sandstone Trail and there is room for a fair few cars. SJ 541715.

DIRECTIONS Barns Bridge Gates car park and this area of Delamere Forest is found within a square south of the M56, west of the A49, north of the A54 and east of the B5393 Helsby to Ashton road. Get on the B5152 Delamere to Frodsham road to reach Hatchmere Village. If approaching from the south turn left after at the crossroads in the village. If coming from the north go right at the same crossroads, once Hatchmere is passed, and drive along this minor road through the forest until the car park is reached on the left a mile or so further on.

BACKGROUND INFORMATION
See page 4

1 Leave the car park going back to the road passing a Sandstone Trail sign. Cross the road carefully taking the Sandstone Trail and entering the forest by walking past a barrier. Curve LEFT at the first path junction staying on The Sandstone Trail. Stay ahead at the next path junction and descend into the woods still on The Sandstone Trail, reaching the woodland edge with clear ground to the right. Continue along the forest edge as the path rises and falls gently before re-entering the forest proper again. Reach a path junction and go straight ahead on a narrower path (The Sandstone Trail) to join another good forest track and go LEFT. Head uphill and curve left past a picnic bench on the left. As the path curves left leave it taking the narrower one ahead still staying with The Sandstone Trail. At a staggered crossroads go RIGHT and almost immediately LEFT crossing The Delamere Loop path. This is still The Sandstone Trail but is not marked at this point. Head downhill steeply to join a small stream on the left-hand side to reach an area of path junctions. Use The Sandstone Trail marker posts to follow the path curving RIGHT and crossing the stream to reach a large Sandstone Trail marker post. Go RIGHT here signposted 'Frodsham', passing a notice board. Rise up steeply into woods and climb to reach a clearer area continuing to reach a barrier on the edge of the forest.

2 Pass the barrier on the left. continuing on a track which rises a little and then descends towards houses to reach a road at Manley Common. Cross the road going half-LEFT taking footpath along a track past houses leaving the Sandstone Trail now, to continue ahead when the track bears sharp left to reach a footpath at a red iron gate. Pass through to follow the right-hand side of the field, climbing near the hedge. Climb steeply to a stile near the top right-hand corner of the field, with good views all around, cross the stile and go immediately RIGHT down the side of the next field to reach a stile. Cross this to exit the field via gates onto a lane. Go LEFT up New Pale Road climbing across the New Pale, and continue, passing the entrance of New Pale Lodge as the road bends left. Straight after this look for gates on the right with a stile to the right of them. Cross the stile taking The Eddisbury Trail and head up the right-hand side of the field, continuing ahead when the hedge on the right ends. Climb to reach a stile and go over it to cross the middle of the next field heading toward a forest ahead. Reach another stile, going through a gap to the right of it and going half-RIGHT over the next field to reach a crossroad of paths at the entrance to the woods.

3 Go ahead along The Eddisbury Way, crossing a stile to walk along a field edge descending to cross a stile. Continue along the right-hand side of a field crossing a stile in the right corner and rising over a field to cross a stile and then cross the lane, continuing over a stile. Go half-RIGHT crossing two stiles. Go

RIGHT to walk through the farmyard to cross a stile near a gate. Go over stepping stones. Pass through a kissing gate and take a green track between fences towards the forest ahead. Pass

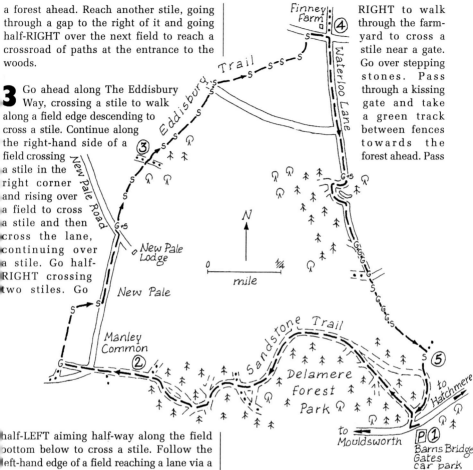

half-LEFT aiming half-way along the field bottom below to cross a stile. Follow the left-hand edge of a field reaching a lane via a stile. Go RIGHT reaching the crossroads after Finney Farm.

4 Go RIGHT along Waterloo Lane), climbing gently to where the lane goes right, going straight on along a green lane, passing a parking area to continue to reach gates and a stile. Cross, taking a track to enter woods via a barrier. Climb the track curving right and left around a pond in a hollow. Continue, going LEFT to a marker post just before a forest track. Keep the pond on your left following the path to a fence at the forest edge. Go RIGHT down the edge of the forest. Reach a farm and pass it via three gates. Continue, passing through a kissing gate beside a gate, and continue towards a house ahead, going LEFT and almost immediately

through two more kissing gates and go over a stile to enter a field. Go half-LEFT uphill passing a marker post, continuing ahead on trackless ground towards a distinct gap in the trees ahead and pass another marker post to walk to a stile in the fence by the forest.

5 Cross the stile to join a track and curve right into the woods and continue to join the blue/white route at a corner, going ahead to curve left and pick up the Sandstone Trail again at a path junction. Go LEFT at this junction to walk to the forest edge and pass a barrier to cross the road and re-enter the car park at Barns Bridge Gates.

HATCHMERE & FLAXMERE

DESCRIPTION Situated on the fringes of the sprawling Forest of Delamere, Hatchmere Lake is a delightful spot for a picnic and a great area for exploring the network of footpaths that surround it. The circuit described below is about 3¾ miles long and will take you about 2½ hours at a leisurely pace, using a combination of forest paths and tracks, bridleways and footpaths and parts of the long distance footpath, The Delamere Way, to complete a large loop around Hatchmere and the dry mere of Flaxmere. It also takes in typical Cheshire farmland and re-enters the forest again to work a way back through the trees and past the lovely Blakemere Moss. This is a great route for all times of the year but it can be wet and muddy in the winter, so wear appropriate footwear and expect a bit of tricky route finding in the early stages.

START There is roadside parking for several cars just outside the village of Hatchmere on the minor road that runs between Hatchmere and Mouldsworth. Park near the barrier across the forest track east of the village (don't block it) and just after the 40mph sign and the village name. SJ 552718.

DIRECTIONS Hatchmere is found within a square south of the M56, west of the A49, north of the A54 and east of the B5393 Helsby to Ashton road. Hatchmere is located on the B5152 Delamere to Frodsham road. If approaching from the south turn left after the forest at the crossroads in the village, if coming from the north go right at the same crossroads once the mere is passed.

BACKGROUND INFORMATION
See page 5

1 Walk back down the road towards the 'Hatchmere' village sign and go LEFT on a footpath into the trees following a woodland path with a fence seen through the trees and with more overgrown forest scenery to the left. As open ground is reached and the tracks bears right, go LEFT to pick up a fainter path that bears slightly right to pass to the right of a solitary oak tree on the edge of the open ground. From there take a faint track half-RIGHT over the marshy cleared area. *THIS NEXT SECTION REQUIRES CONCENTRATION TO GET THE ROUTE CORRECT!* Reach a T-junction of paths near trees ahead and go LEFT to walk up to a marker post (yellow arrow) and here go RIGHT on a good path through the trees, which you follow with a fence on your left, as it works a way through the forest. At a finger post go RIGHT over a bridge and continue by the side of a brook, curving right to cross another bridge. Follow the path towards a house ahead and follow the fence around it keeping it to your left as you continue around the house curving left to head towards a road. Just before a gate and the road go RIGHT when the track splits to continue alongside the mere on your right to walk to a road.

2 Cross the road going RIGHT along the pavement, with Hatchmere over to the right, walking towards The Carriers Inn. A little before it, just after Hatchmere Farm go LEFT up a bridleway signposted 'Norley Road and School Lane'. Stay LEFT when it splits (signposted Norley Road) on the better track, with Flaxmere dry mere down to the right. Curve right around the back of a pale-yellow house and continue ahead to take the bridleway RIGHT (blue arrow) by Flax Moss Cottage, going half-RIGHT towards the white cottage and going RIGHT in front of it to go LEFT around it on a good track. Go to the RIGHT of Bell House, going half-LEFT to pick up the access drive for it and walk along it to a T-junction of tracks. Go LEFT heading towards School Lane to reach a road. Cross School Lane and head along Post Office Lane for about twenty metres to take a bridleway on the RIGHT by a gate. Pass through the gate to walk down a green lane towards a farm. Pass through a gate into the farmyard curving right on a farm access track (a Permissive Path) to go LEFT just before the house and behind farm buildings, continuing up the concrete drive to pass on to a green lane and exit onto a field. Stay near the hedge to descend into the bottom left-hand corner of the grassy meadow to pass through a gate and continue along the left-hand side of the

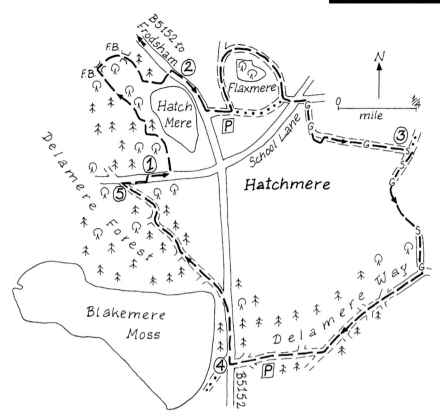

next field, turning LEFT in the bottom corner to reach a stile.

3 Cross the stile and go RIGHT and uphill on The Delamere Way to pass through a gate. Walk along the side of the field to pass through another gate. Now go half-LEFT over the large field (trackless at first) to pick up a cart track and curve left picking up a fence on the left, following it and going RIGHT when the track spits. Pass under a large oak tree, heading for the right of two gates ahead to cross a stile in the corner and continue on a good track to pass through another gate to reach a rough lane. Go RIGHT (Delamere Loop and Delamere Way) climbing to enter Delamere Forest proper via bollards. Go straight on and downhill, dropping to stay RIGHT at a path junction, staying in the hollow and curving left, to go RIGHT at the next path junction, climbing steeply uphill on a good track. Follow this track, ignoring minor turns left or right, to descend, climb up again and finally go RIGHT when it splits to enter a large car park. Walk straight down it towards the road ahead. Pass a barrier to cross the road and reach a second barrier on the other side.

4 Pass the barrier, descending towards Blakemere Moss, curving right to pick up the Red route and follow it along with the mere curving left into the forest after a barrier. When the track goes left stay straight on (Red route) to climb steeply to a T-junction near a bench. Here go RIGHT on the White/Blue route going straight on at a junction to pass a barrier and reach the road.

5 Turn RIGHT down the road using the forest edges to walk along, staying off the tarmac. Just before the Hatchmere sign carefully cross over back to your car.

13

WALK 6

EXPLORING DELAMERE FOREST

DESCRIPTION Delamere Forest is a criss-cross network of tracks, paths and narrow forest trods. There are a number of colour-marked forest trails, and both The Sandstone Trail and The Baker Way pass through the woodland, with plenty of scope for exploration. The forest is a firm favourite with local people and also attracts many day visitors from the surrounding towns and cities. For families it provides a great way to introduce children to the joys of the great outdoors. The 5 mile circuit described below explores a large portion of the forest, linking up the coloured forest trails and the long distance footpaths to show the very best of what this area has to offer. Allow 3 hours.

START From Linmere Lodge car park and Forest Visitor Centre (pay and display). SJ 549704.

DIRECTIONS Linmere Lodge car park is located next to the Forest Visitor Centre and is reached via a minor lane that leaves the B5152 near Delamere Station (it is signposted). The B5152 runs between Frodsham and Delamere/Oakmere. If approaching from Frodsham turn right just after Delamere Station, if coming from Delamere/Oakmere direction go left just before the station.

BACKGROUND INFORMATION
See page 5

I Head out of the car park following signs for 'Forest Trails' and 'Go Ape' passing the cycle hire and walking towards the bridge ahead. Go LEFT at the top of the bridge to enter the forest, going immediately RIGHT following The Blakemere Trail (Red route) and signs for 'Go Ape'. Curve right on the Red route going left of the 'Go Ape' building and continuing ahead on a good wide track, rising up to curve slightly left and then bend right to reach a T-junction near the waters of Blakemere Moss. Go RIGHT on the Red route walking along the edge of Blakemere

Moss and going RIGHT when the path splits, climbing to pass a forest barrier (leaving Red route now) and cross a road continuing ahead on the opposite side, walking up into a car park. Exit this in the top right-hand corner passing a black/yellow barrier and following a good forest track (Yellow arrow). Go straight on at crossroads to curve left and pass a junction and a bench. Reach a major path crossroads going straight over and staying LEFT at the next junction to climb up a grooved sandy path to reach a fence and sign for 'The Delamere Way'

2 Go LEFT downhill keeping to the left of the fence. Stay RIGHT when the track splits, climbing uphill by the fence and descending to a boggy hollow. Stay RIGHT when it splits again to curve left next to a stream at the forest edge. Follow the path keeping the stream to the right and following the forest edge. This narrow path, which is boggy after rain, continues by the stream to reach a crossroads of paths by a bridge. Continue straight on with the stream still on the right. The path is wider now – follow it alongside the stream, walking ahead when it splits, keeping beside the stream. As you reach a road leave the stream, curving left and staying in the woods with the road on the right. Go RIGHT at a small crossroads to reach the road, crossing over it to reach a black/yellow barrier near Blakemere Moss.

3 Pass by the barrier, curving left on the good forest track, going LEFT at the first major junction to stay alongside Blakemere Moss. Keep ahead at the next junction (Blue/White marker) to pick up the Red route again at a crossroads of paths, curving left around the head of Blakemere Moss. By a picnic bench and path junction, go RIGHT following the Red route by sculptures and winding uphill to climb to a T-junction where you go RIGHT on The Sandstone Trail. Stay on this good path to pass by a barrier and reach a road near the car park at Barns Bridge Gates. Cross the road going slightly right to reach a

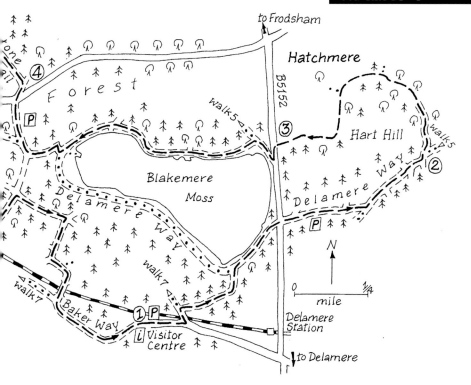

barrier at the start of a forest track.

4 Pass the barrier, still on The Sandstone Trail, to re-enter the woods on the Blue route, going LEFT as the track splits staying on The Sandstone Trail and picking up the White route. At the next junction go LEFT, leaving The Sandstone Trail and following the White route. Continue on the good track and when it goes sharp right leave the White route to go ahead on a smaller path and follow this, ignoring any turnings off it, until it narrows and you reach a good forest track at a T-junction. Go LEFT and downhill to pass a barrier and reach the road. Cross, re-entering the woods via a barrier and go immediately RIGHT to descend steeply on a path through the woods. Curve left over a brook and climb steeply up the other side to reach a railway bridge.

5 Cross the bridge, staying LEFT once over to pick up The Baker Way, climbing uphill into trees. The path levels out to curve right where you continue to reach a T-junction. Curve left and stay on The Baker Way. Reach a railway bridge and cross it again, continuing ahead on The Baker Way to reach The Sandstone Trail at a T-junction. Go LEFT to reach a major crossroads near a sign for 'The Hunger Hill Trail'. Here go RIGHT, continuing to the next major crossroads and going RIGHT to pick up the Green route. Walk along this to reach a path junction, where you go LEFT following Red/Green routes to curve right past a bench to cross a third railway bridge. Curve right and go LEFT at the next junction following the Red/Green route (just before a bench on the right). Descend into a hollow, climb out the other side and follow the path to exit the forest through bollards at a lane. Go LEFT along the pathway and walk past a white house to reach The Visitor Centre and car park.

15

EDDISBURY HILL

DESCRIPTION The communications mast on Pale Heights, the summit of Eddisbury Hill, is visible for miles around the Cheshire Plain. This 4½ mile route climbs over the top of the hill on excellent paths, before dropping down into Delamere Forest and following trails through it to make a return over Eddisbury Hill back to your car. Allow 3 hours.

START From Gresty's Waste car park (free) near Kelsall. SJ 540686.

DIRECTIONS Gresty's Waste car park is a staging post on the Sandstone Trail. It offers plenty of parking space and is free. It is located on the A54 near its junction with the A556 between Kelsall and the Delamere/Oakmere area. From Chester use the A51 picking up the A54 near Tarvin. The car park will be found on the right, a little further on from the traffic lights at the top of Kelsall Hill. From Manchester direction, the A556 can be followed and the car park will be on the left just after the A54 joins. Note the exit from the car park carefully as it is difficult to get clear views of the road.

BACKGROUND INFORMATION
See page 18

1 Leave the car park following The Sandstone Trail through woods. This bends RIGHT to reach the road. Cross (*be careful with children – this is a busy road*) and head into Nettleford Woods (signposted Barnsbridge Gates/visitor centre) entering woods to pass to the left of a barrier and heading uphill on a good track. Continue to climb until a crossroad of paths is reached with a signpost for 'Pale Heights/Sandstone Trail Alternative' and here go RIGHT. Follow the good track through two hedge gaps going RIGHT after the second to climb uphill to pass through a fence and join a metalled lane to the right of the masts.

2 Go straight ahead on the lane joining another lane and in a short distance go LEFT on a track between wire fences to reach a T-junction of paths with a bench on the left. Go RIGHT to pass another bench and descend to curve left to enter a plantation. Follow the path downhill eventually crossing a stream in a hollow and then zigzag more steeply downhill to reach a T-junction of tracks by a marker post. Here go RIGHT on the track, forking LEFT just before telegraph wires. A little further on go LEFT again just before a lane to pass to the right of a wooden sign and continue past a white boulder to descend to a kissing gate.

3 Pass through the kissing gate, going LEFT up the lane and then RIGHT over the railway bridge by a coloured marked post to enter Delamere Forest proper, after houses on the left, and passing a barrier. (If you want to go to visitor centre go ahead, not right, at this point). A forest track winds through the trees to arrive at a crossroad of paths. Go LEFT here and continue to a T-junction of paths facing a red and green marker post. Here go LEFT and continue straight on to pass a bench and curve right to cross a railway bridge. Curve right again, passing another bench to continue through the woods on a good path that finally descends before climbing up sharply to a fence gap on the LEFT as the path bears right.

4 Go LEFT through the gap on The Sandstone Trail following the path, with a stream on the right, to pass through a gap to reach a rough road. Here, go LEFT on The Sandstone Trail, passing Eddisbury Lodge Carry on ahead when The Sandstone Trail goes off right and follow the lane. When the hedge on the left ends near a gate, take the track on the RIGHT, passing the barrier and climbing up steeply to reach a bench on the right.

5 Carry on uphill and, at a path junction with the masts up to the left, take the RIGHT-hand track (with a Sandstone Trail marker) following it and passing through two hedges as you pick up your outbound route to descend to Nettleford Woods Go LEFT (signposted Gresty's Waste and Primrose Hill) and descend to cross the road again (*carefully*) and go LEFT to walk through the woods back to the car park.

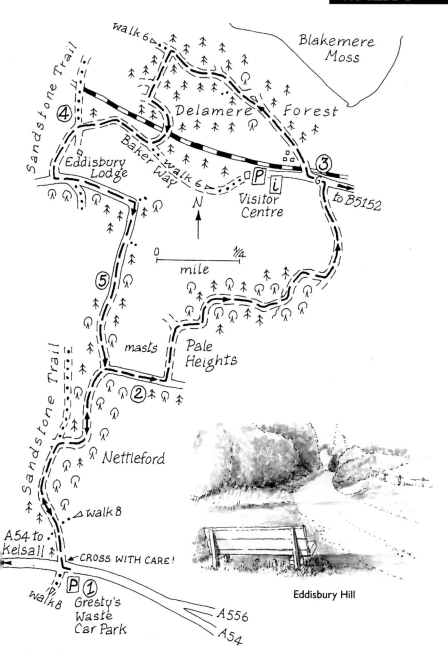

Blakemere Moss

walk 6

Sandstone Trail

Delamere Forest

④

Eddisbury Lodge

Baker Way

walk 6

③

P i

Visitor Centre

to B5152

N

0 ¼ mile

⑤

masts

Pale Heights

②

Sandstone Trail

Nettleford

△ walk 8

A54 to Kelsall

CROSS WITH CARE!

P ①

walk 8

Gresty's Waste Car Park

A556

A54

Eddisbury Hill

The Whitegate Way. Walks 11 & 12

WALK 7
EDDISBURY HILL

There is a really useful network of paths over Pale Heights and the summit of Eddisbury Hill, and walkers have a choice of routes. Good car parks are found at both Gresty's Waste and in Delamere Forest near the Visitor Centre. The summit area is a popular viewpoint with benches and far-reaching views. As it rises above the surrounding plain you can see as far as the Clwydian Hills of North Wales and the Peak District to the east on a clear day, as well as being able to pick out the two cathedrals in the city of Liverpool. There are the remains of an Iron Age hillfort on the summit, and some of the larger earth works and ditches are still visible – this is the largest of Cheshire's Iron Age hilltop forts.

WALK 8
WATLING STREET

Watling Street was the road the Romans built to link Chester to Manchester, and the final section of this route follows the line of it across the fields from Stoney Lane. None of it is visible now but it would have provided a straight line for the legions to move troops and provisions in the days when few roads of any description existed. Gresty's Waste Car park is situated on the A54, which was an old turnpike road, travellers using it would have been required to stop at the cottage near the car park to pay a toll.

WALK 9
KELSALL HILL & KELSALL VILLAGE

This walk follows the Eddisbury Way steeply up to the lovely viewpoint of Kelsall Hill. This is open access land but it is best to keep to the network of paths. The views west are stunning and on a clear day you can see as far as Liverpool with its Cathedrals, as well as to the Mersey Estuary.

Kelsall is set prettily on the foothills of the Sandstone Ridge and since the A54 was by-passed it is has become secluded and quiet. The by-pass is two miles long and cost £3.8 million pounds, and was opened in 1986. The route followed crosses it twice.

Kelsall is located eight miles east of Chester and eight miles west of Northwich and has four pubs for those in need of refreshment or food.

WALK 10
BUDWORTH COMMON

A lot of the tracks and paths over and around Little Budworth Common are of ancient origin, and would have been in use as far back as Norman times when this area would have been an outlying part o the hunting woodland of Mara and Mondrem. Bu the heathland here has its true origins even furthe back than this as this since, like all heathland, i was forest cleared by Stone Age man and used fo grazing animals. Common heather is the main plan seen on heathland, and wild country such as Littl Budworth Common also provides a regular habita for many species of birds, insects and most of ou larger mammals.

BACKGROUND INFORMATION

WALKS 11 & 12
WHITEGATE WAY

The 6 miles of the Whitegate Way route that can be followed on this route was originally a railway, opened on 1st June 1870. Its purpose was to transport salt from the mines at Winsford and take a direct course to join the main line between Chester and Manchester at Cuddington, where the salt could be freighted on to its final destinations. The line closed in 1966. During its 96-year life it also transported passengers intermittently but this was never a great success and the line remained primarily a salt line.

The final reminders of the old line are seen at Whitegate Station where the platform is located and a loading gauge is still visible. But these aside, all is now given over to recreation in the form of walking and horse riding. The Whitegate Way is also popular with joggers and bike riders. Cheshire County Council publish an informative leaflet entitled 'Whitegate Way' – email: whitegateway@cheshire.gov.uk for further details.

WALK 13
CASTLES

Of the two castles seen on the walk, the most dramatic and oldest is Beeston. Set in an easily defended position it is a prominent landmark for miles around and dates from the period between 1220 and 1230 when it was built by the then Earl of Chester – one Randle De Blunderville. It saw battle in the English Civil War.

Peckforton Castle is now a popular hotel and is much more recent in origin. Dating from about 1850 it was built and designed by Anthony Salvin for the very first Lord Tollermache in a distinctly Mediaeval style. This has made it popular with film makers looking for sets for movies and for television shows that are period pieces.

WALKS 14
BULKELEY HILL

Bulkeley Hill comes as a bit of a surprise to walkers in West Cheshire. From the end of Coppermines Line most are tempted to head for Raw Head (the highest point in West Cheshire) but when they take The Sandstone Trail east from this point instead of west, they get a pleasant surprise. Locals have known the delights of Bulkeley Hill for years and it is a regular spot for dog walkers and families bringing children for a romp on a Sunday afternoon. It is a hill walk that will both delight and entertain.

Bulkeley Hill is owned mostly by the National Trust covering 87 acres (35 hectares). If you venture off the paths (and even if you don't) you will often find evidence of an old water pumping system and hilltop reservoir that still exists here. Tramlines vanish up the hillside and leave you wondering why, and watch out for the abundant bird life and the very old, twisted, sweet chestnut trees that were originally used to provide timber for local fencing.

The reservoir on the hilltop is not easy to see but is still in use and provides water by gravity to the villages on the plain below. The tramline puzzle is solved when you learn that they were put in to aid the supply of equipment to the reservoir surge regulator in 1949.

WALK 15
RAW HEAD SUMMIT

At 277 metres Raw Head's sandstone outcrop summit is the highest point in West Cheshire. Riddled with old workings and caves it is a fascinating area to explore. However, the real attraction here is the view. Clear days give up to 30 miles visibility in most directions but it is most limited to the east. The Clwydian Hills of North Wales and the Shropshire Hills to the south are all in view from either the summit or the view-points along the ridge itself.

WALK 8

GRESTY'S WASTE & PRIMROSEHILL WOOD

DESCRIPTION This entertaining circuit of 6 miles explores the undulating countryside around the area known as Gresty's Waste and the woodland and pathways of Primrosehill Wood. There is a vast network of paths in this region and the route links together the best of them to give a good circular walk that uses The Sandstone Trail, good tracks and footpaths, some road walking and forest trails complete the circuit. This is a rough and tumble outing that will require good boots. It will take about 3½ hours.

START From Gresty's Waste car park (free) near Kelsall. SO 593775.

DIRECTIONS Gresty's Waste car park is a staging post on the Sandstone Trail and offers plenty of parking space and is free. It is located on the A54 near its junction with the A556 between Kelsall and the Delamere/Oakmere area. From Chester use the A51 picking up the A54 near Tarvin and the car park will be found on the right a little further on from the traffic lights at the top of Kelsall Hill. From Manchester direction, the A556 can be followed and the car park will be on the left just after the A54 joins left. Note the exit from the car park carefully as it is difficult to get clear views of the road.

BACKGROUND INFORMATION
See page 18

I Leave the car park following The Sandstone Trail through woods. with the road to the right, and continuing with it when the path splits, to bear left and descend steeply down wooden steps to cross a brook via a bridge. Curve right on the opposite side to climb half RIGHT up through the woods. Leave the trees as the angle eases to curve left along an avenue of trees and cross two stiles in quick succession over a track. A little further on cross another two stiles over another track. Stay on The Sandstone Trail to climb up on a good path bearing left and then right into Primrosehill Wood. Pass through woodland on a good sandy path climbing gradually to eventually descend on a wide path to join a track at a corner in the woods. Follow The Sandstone Trail going LEFT (and ignoring the immediate first left) and descend for a short distance going RIGHT at a crossroads of paths to stay on The Sandstone Trail. Climb uphill to reach a fingerpost and kissing gate on the RIGHT, going through it to ascend the right hand side of the field curving right to pass through another kissing gate (still on the Sandstone Trail) and go LEFT up the next field passing through another two kissing gates to pass to the left of a café to exit onto a lane via a stile.

2 Go LEFT on the lane and in a short distance, as the lane bears LEFT, leave it to go RIGHT on The Sandstone Trail signposted 'Beeston'. Follow this good track as it descends (with a little bit of ascent) all the way to pass by a metal gate and reach a road. Go LEFT up the road to pass Rock Farm and continue ahead when The Sandstone Trail leaves to the right. Continue on the road to pass a farm and descend to reach a farm access lane on the left by a Public Footpath sign for 'Tirley Lane'.

3 Go LEFT along the access lane and just before a 'Private Road' sign, go RIGHT following the footpath sign for Tirley Lane and passing through a gate to enter woodland on a good track. Curve left on this and follow it through the woods, ascending (with a little bit of descent) all the way to the end to exit onto a lane via a gate. Go RIGHT along this lane (Tirley Lane) to pass Tirley Farm and curve left at crossroads going ahead to follow the edge of Primrosehill Woods and reach a stile on the left as the woods end. Cross this and follow an indistinct path steeply downhill near the edge of woods. The path soon becomes better and descends through the woodland keeping close to the right-hand edge of it before climbing over the wooded heights of Harrow Hill. Once over keep ahead and descend by the forest edge until you are close to the gate that marks the edge of the woodland. Here look for a fainter path on the left into the woods and take it, to eventually reach a forest track at a bend. Go RIGHT, following the track into the woods eventually rising up and curving left. Here watch for a turning on the RIGHT. Take it to descend through woodland. As the track bends left look for a stile on the right signposted 'South Hill'.

4 Cross the stile, and another straight after. Go diagonally right across the meadow aiming for the top right-hand corner of the field. Cross three stiles before exiting the field via a final stile and passing through a gap to the left of gates. Carefully cross the road and walk down Stoney Lane to cross another busy road to the right of the school on the opposite side. Follow Stoney Lane uphill and continuing when the houses end, to arrive at a stile on the left close to few houses.

5 Go LEFT over the stile to follow the top right-hand edge of the field roughly in line with where the old Roman road used to be (see page 18). Pass through a gate opening to continue for some distance along the field edge to cross a stile in the field corner and go straight ahead along a narrow path to curve left to cross a stile and enter Nettleford Wood. Descend on the path to reach a good track at a crossroads and go LEFT on The Sandstone Trail again, following it to pass around a barrier by a house, to reach a road. Cross carefully and bear left in the woods to walk back to your car.

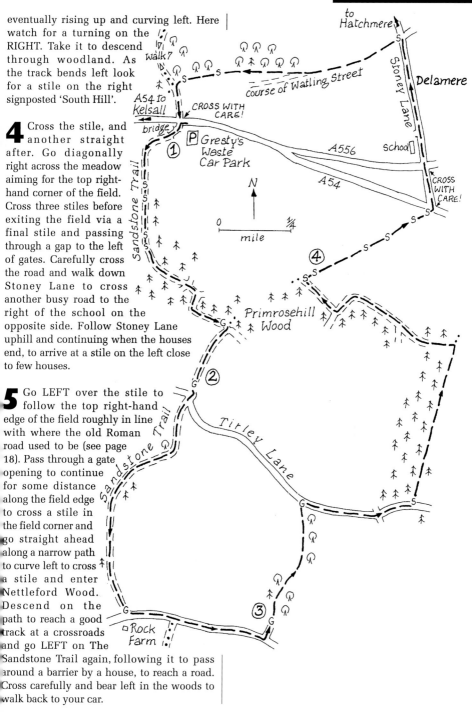

KELSALL & THE SANDSTONE FOOTHILLS

DESCRIPTION The pretty Cheshire village of Kelsall is located on a hillside with extensive views of west Cheshire and the Welsh border hills, amidst a maze of footpaths which can be linked and joined to give a great circuit of 5 miles, exploring the sandstone foothills of the great sandstone ridge. The route described starts and ends at the little known car park of Brine's Brow on the western fringes of the Forest of Delamere, and uses stretches of both The Eddisbury Way and The Baker Way. Some of the sections can be muddy, and a time of 2½ – 3 hours is suggested for the outing.

START Brine's Brow car park on the western fringes of Delamere Forest. The car park is a decent sized one but can be affected by closures in the winter months, so check by calling 01606 882167. If the barrier is down there is space for a car or two on the grass verge alongside but please park carefully and be sure not to block the road or the nearby junction. SJ 524708.

DIRECTIONS Brine's Brow car park is located down minor roads and can be reached by using the A54 Chester to Kelsall road, leaving it to enter the village of Kelsall. From here you will need to use a road atlas and head north on a minor road that starts near the Post Office and the church and passes under the A54 Kelsall by-pass and continues for about 2½ miles or so to reach Brine's Brow, which is located by going right at the first proper crossroad reached.

BACKGROUND INFORMATION
See page 18

I Leave the car park, heading south to pass the Delamere Forest Park sign on the right and enter the picnic area, walking through it and going to the left of a pond to pick up a path and stay RIGHT when it splits to pass close to a picnic table and reach a fence on the right to continue uphill and join a track in the forest, going RIGHT along it to pass a barrier and reach a lane. Go LEFT along it (The Eddisbury Way) continuing to go RIGHT on a footpath after a farm access track. Cross a stile to go half-LEFT (still on The Eddisbury Way) following the yellow arrows to walk over a field to a track. Here go RIGHT and cross a stile going half-LEFT over the next field, passing to the right of the first telegraph pole on a faint path, to cross a stile amongst high conifers. Walk through the trees and go LEFT down the left-hand edge of the field. Stay on the Eddisbury Way and follow the marker arrows to walk along the left-hand edges of a series of fields. Finally cross a track and go to the left of a big hedge and curve left around a meadow following the field edge to leave the path and exit LEFT through a hedge and wall gap to reach a lane. Go RIGHT to follow the lane, and, when the wood ends, cross to the left-hand side of the lane, using the wide verge to walk to a kissing gate on the left, just after a white house on the right.

2 Go LEFT through the kissing gate, following the Eddisbury Way steeply uphill, curving to the right of a tree and heading to top corner of the field. Climb steps to pass through a kissing gate to follow the path half-LEFT on the edge of the next field. Go RIGHT just before a hedge gap, following arrows and keeping the hedge on the left. Continue ahead through the next field gap, keeping the hedge on the left to reach a crossroads of paths in a corner near a pond. Follow yellow arrows to enter the next field and walk across it on a track to exit via a stile to reach the A54. Cross via break in central barrier (*take care!*) to pick up a path on the other side, walking down a short track to enter a field via a stile and head across the field to pass through a kissing gate and follow the track beyond. As it curves left go ahead to pass through a kissing gate and follow The Eddisbury Way down a narrow track between hedges to reach gates. Pass through the small one on the RIGHT to reach Brooms Lane. Go RIGHT down the lane (still The Eddisbury Way) and, when it splits in front of Cross Lanes Cottage, go RIGHT following Grub Lane and descending steeply. When it splits near the bottom turn RIGHT in front of the Methodist Church passing the war memorial on the right, then curving right to reach a road. Turn RIGHT along it

Continue until the road curves right. Here go LEFT on a footpath beside Orchard Mount House to follow a sunken track downhill to cross a stile into a field. Curve right around the bottom of the field following marker arrows to turn LEFT. Descend to cross a stile and join a lane.

3 Turn RIGHT along the lane and continue until it bends left. Here go **⑤** ahead to pick up a footpath to the left of Northwood Caravan Site and pass a football field. Follow this green track to cross a stile, ascend steps and re-cross the A54 via a gap in the central barrier (*again being very careful*). Pick up a footpath on the other side to descend steps, cross a stile and enter a field. Walk down the left-hand edge of field to cross a bridge via two stiles and continue on the left-hand edge of next field to cross another stile in the left corner of the field. Continue to cross two more stiles, descend steps and pick up a green track. Go LEFT down it to exit onto a lane near houses at Ashton Hayes. Go straight on, ignoring turnings left and right, and then curve left to reach a road at a T-junction.

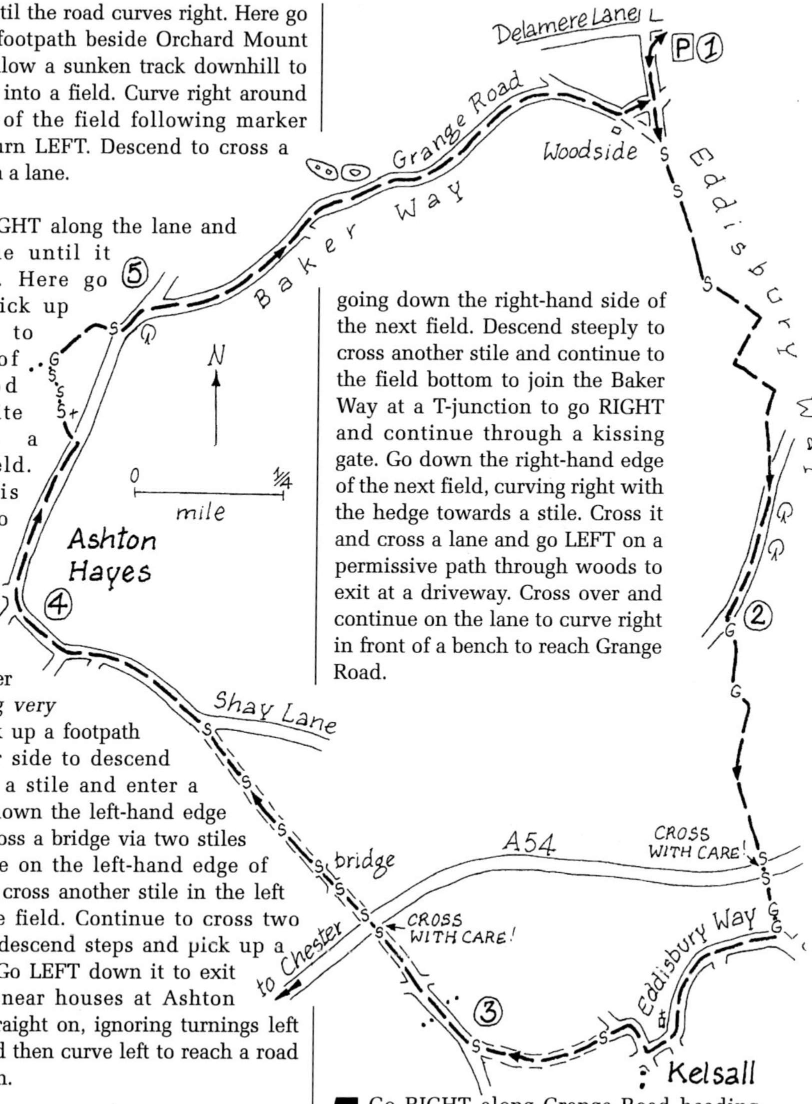

4 Turn RIGHT, continuing to another junction, and going right again to cross over the road and walk towards the church ahead. Pass a school and continue to go LEFT at the church entrance by a footpath sign. Walk to the left of the church, going right up the steps by the door, to go LEFT and RIGHT of the church following yellow arrows through the churchyard to exit in the bottom left-hand corner via a stile and going half-RIGHT down the field to cross a stile and

going down the right-hand side of the next field. Descend steeply to cross another stile and continue to the field bottom to join the Baker Way at a T-junction to go RIGHT and continue through a kissing gate. Go down the right-hand edge of the next field, curving right with the hedge towards a stile. Cross it and cross a lane and go LEFT on a permissive path through woods to exit at a driveway. Cross over and continue on the lane to curve right in front of a bench to reach Grange Road.

5 Go RIGHT along Grange Road heading uphill to pass the entrance to Ashton Grange and then descend on the lane (still on The Baker Way) to pass fishing ponds. Climb again and continue, passing a cottage and finally reaching a T-junction. Go RIGHT, and, just before Woodside Farm, go LEFT on a footpath into trees, continuing to exit onto a road. Cross over the road passing the barrier to enter Brine's Brow picnic area. Go immediately LEFT back to the picnic area and the car park.

Map labels: Delamere Lane, P①, Grange Road, Baker Way, Woodside, Eddisbury Way, ②, N, 0 ¼ mile, Ashton Hayes, ④, Shay Lane, bridge, A54, CROSS WITH CARE!, CROSS WITH CARE!, to Chester, ③, Eddisbury Way, Kelsall

EXPLORING LITTLE BUDWORTH COMMON & COUNTRY PARK

DESCRIPTION Little Budworth Country Park adjoins the race circuit of Oulton Park, and the route described below returns to the start along the edges of it. With that in mind, make sure you DON'T time your visit to coincide with a race meeting (usually held on Bank Holidays), as it gets very noisy here and the whole tranquil nature of the walk would be spoilt. The circuit outlined is 5 miles long and mostly on the level, making use of the extensive network of footpaths, bridleways, green lanes and marked routes. There are wonderful woods and a variety of surprising and unexpected green tracks and hidden hollows. If you allow 3 hours you will enjoy a relaxing walk through an area of Cheshire not known to a lot of visitors.

START From Little Budworth Country Park car park (no fee and toilets plus height restriction for taller vehicles) at SJ 590654 near the junction of two minor roads a little to the west of Little Budworth Village and near the gates of Oulton Park race circuit.

DIRECTIONS Little Budworth Country Park car park is best found by heading for Little Budworth village and following signs for 'Oulton Park Race Track'. If you imagine a square using the B5074 Nantwich to Winsford road, the A54 between Winsford and Kelsall, the A51 between Nantwich and Tarporley and the A49 between Tarporley and Cuddington, Little Budworth is located near the top north-west corner. Once at Little Budworth village, drive out towards the race circuit and, as the first walls and gate of the circuit are reached on the left, take the minor road to the right. The car park is on the right just after you turn. It may be tricky to locate, but if you can't seem to find it ask in the village for directions.

BACKGROUND INFORMATION
See page 18

1 Exit the car park, crossing straight over the road to take a track onto the heath. Reach a T-junction of paths and go RIGHT, curving left to follow a good track over Little Budworth Common. Stay on the track ignoring any minor turns off it to go over a crossroads of paths (with the main gates of Oulton Park to the left) and continue to curve right to reach a major path crossroads where you stay ahead (the Delamere Loop goes right and left) following footpath arrows. Continue through the trees to reach a forest track at the edge of the woods. Cross this, still following the yellow arrows, to pass through a fence gap keeping near the woods edge. At a minor split go to the RIGHT, heading towards a finger post to go half-LEFT (red arrow) and continue close to the edge of the trees with more open ground to the left. Finally reach a wide track near a footpath sign (no. 71).

2 Go RIGHT to walk down the track (muddy after rain) to reach a road. Cross over and head down Beech Road. Continue past two footpaths going off right and, once the forest ends on the right, continue ahead on the lane to reach a footpath and stile near a house. Cross the stile heading down the right-hand side of the field to reach a gate and stile, cross and walk down the right-hand side of the next field to reach another stile and gate. Cross the stile and descend on a good track, in a deep valley. Reach a T-junction of paths to go RIGHT with a pond on the left, continuing past another pond to reach a crossroads near a signpost. Curve LEFT just before the sign to follow the track uphill climbing the sunken lane to another junction of paths going straight on (The Delamere Loop), and continuing uphill to join a lane after some houses. Walk along the lane for a short distance to reach a right turn just before a cream house.

3 Go RIGHT down the lane and, as it bears right, go LEFT onto the footpath and 'Restricted Byway' at the footpath sign. Follow the track to a T-junction and go RIGHT on a wide green track, which is surfaced after a short while. Curve left with it and reach a road. Go RIGHT for a few metres and then cross and go LEFT down the green lane. At a field entrance carry on ahead taking a path between the fields. This turns into a wider track and descends with Little Budworth Mere below right. Continue to cross a stile on the RIGHT by a footpath sign, going down the field to cross a second stile. Go RIGHT of the fence to cross a third stile near the Mere. Turn LEFT following the path beside the Mere to cross a stile and reach a road. Go RIGHT, up the road, walking into Little Budworth and, as the road bends right by the church, go LEFT down a lane, then immediately RIGHT up St Peters Drive through houses. At end of the drive curve right to take a footpath on the LEFT, passing between houses to reach a stile.

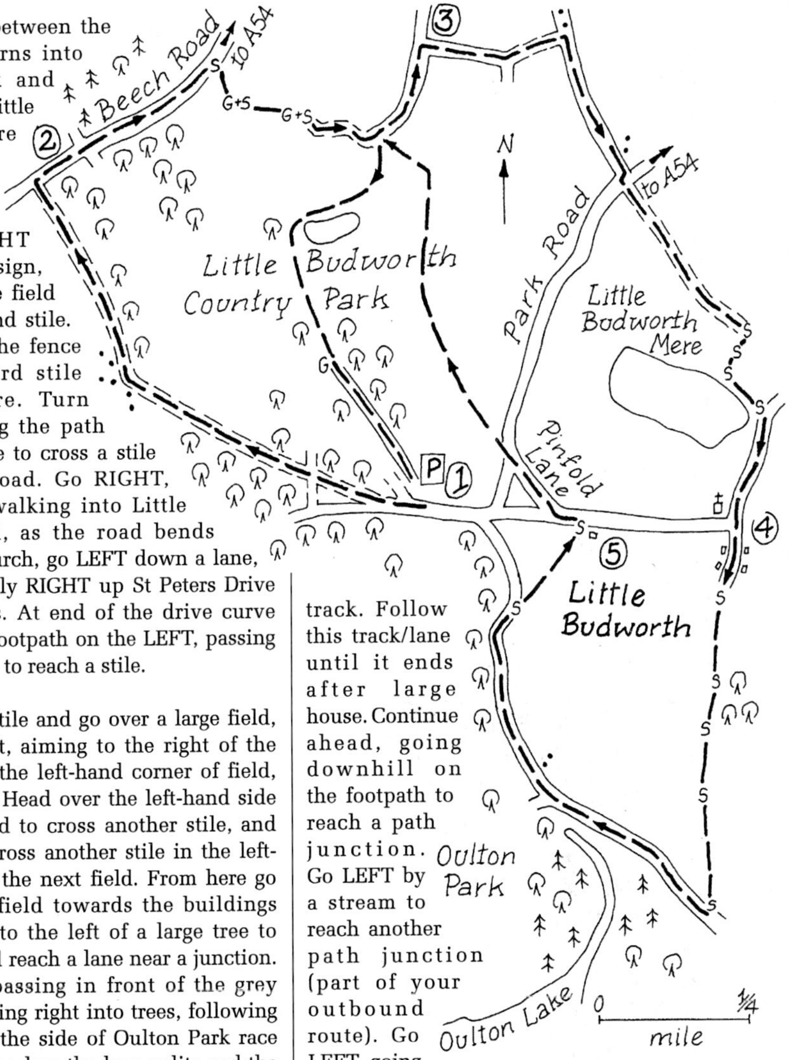

4 Cross the stile and go over a large field, veering left, aiming to the right of the little woods at the left-hand corner of field, to cross a stile. Head over the left-hand side of the next field to cross another stile, and continuing to cross another stile in the left-hand corner of the next field. From here go over the next field towards the buildings ahead, aiming to the left of a large tree to cross a stile and reach a lane near a junction. Turn RIGHT, passing in front of the grey house and curving right into trees, following the lane down the side of Oulton Park race track. Stay right when the lane splits and the wall bends left, and carry on down the lane until a stile is reached at the top of a small rise. Go half-RIGHT over the stile to cross the field, going left of a fence and hedge and exiting over a stile to reach a road near a building.

5 Go LEFT for a short distance, then RIGHT at the War Memorial, and walk down Pinfold Lane passing pub on the right. At the end of the lane cross over, going slightly right, to pick up a footpath along a good track. Follow this track/lane until it ends after large house. Continue ahead, going downhill on the footpath to reach a path junction. Go LEFT by a stream to reach another path junction (part of your outbound route). Go LEFT, going to the left of a pond to climb up through the woods to reach more open ground. Continue on the track, curving to the left, to re-enter the woodland at the Country Park. When the fence ends carry straight on to reach a crossroads of paths (The Delamere Loop) where you turn LEFT on a forest track. Follow the Red route passing to the left of a gate and staying near the left-hand edge of the woods to finally curve right and then left and re-enter the car park.

Little Budworth Country Park

Little Budworth Mere

Park Road

to A54

Beech Road

to A54

Pinfold Lane

Little Budworth

Oulton Park

Oulton Lake

0   ¼   mile

TWO SHORT WALKS ALONG WHITEGATE WAY

DESCRIPTION Stretching for 6 miles from the salt town of Winsford to the Cheshire village of Cuddington, the old railway track now known as The Whitegate Way is probably the furthest this book ventures from the area around the Sandstone Ridge, but as it runs almost to Delamere Forest it deserves its place in this guide. The first route, around Newchurch Common, is just over 2½ miles long and will take about 1½ hours and the second, circling the deep hollow of Marton Hole, is 2 miles and can be done in a little over an hour – of course you can take as long as you like – The Whitegate Way is made for leisurely exploration and there are many benches to rest on along the way.

START Both routes start and finish at the old Whitegate Station where there is a free car park, picnic benches and toilets. SJ 615679.

DIRECTIONS The Old Station car park is almost the central point on the old Whitegate railway line, and is an ideal starting point for walking in the area. It is best found by first getting to the town of Winsford using the A54 and heading west until the roundabout on the outskirts of town, where the A54 goes to the south. Here go straight ahead for a short distance on a minor road to reach Salterswall at a bend in the road. Go left down the minor road in the direction of Sandiway. At the bottom of the hill turn left at the junction and continue up the lane to the first crossroads, ignoring a turning to the right before you reach it. At the crossroads go left to reach traffic lights and, as you pass through them, cross the bridge and go immediately back left to drive past the old station house and into the car park.

BACKGROUND INFORMATION
See page 19

1 NEWCHURCH COMMON

1 Exit the car park onto the old railway line (now a bridleway and footpath) going LEFT along it and passing the old station, going under a bridge to continue as signposted Cuddington and Delamere Forest, and staying LEFT at a path junction and ignoring any turnings right or left. Pass a caravan site and carry on ahead to pass a bench and go around a wooden barrier to reach the large crossroads at Newchurch Crossing.

2 Go ahead (signposted Cuddington and Delamere Forest) to pass another barrier and continue a short distance to go RIGHT through a fence opening towards the old Marton Quarry (now flooded) on Newchurch Common. Go immediately LEFT, following the path around the lake and curving right to reach a stile by a barrier. Cross it, continue ahead for a short way to cross another stile and exit onto a rough lane. Go RIGHT and walk between the two lakes to reach a path crossroads beyond the lake.

3 Take the path RIGHT into the woods, staying LEFT at a path junction, and near the end of the open ground on the right, curve left back into the woods to join a track at a T-junction. Here go RIGHT to

26

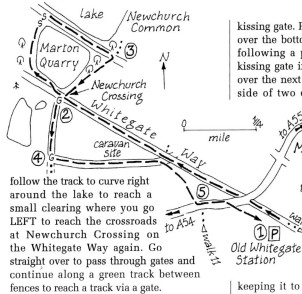

follow the track to curve right around the lake to reach a small clearing where you go LEFT to reach the crossroads at Newchurch Crossing on the Whitegate Way again. Go straight over to pass through gates and continue along a green track between fences to reach a track via a gate.

4 Go LEFT on a restricted byway to follow a lane and pass through gate opening by 10mph sign, continuing ahead to pass a house, a farm and a caravan site. Finally pass a stables and curve right to walk to the end of the lane.

5 Turn LEFT along the road, crossing to walk past houses on the right-hand side. Just before traffic lights go half-RIGHT down the lane and back into the station car park.

2 A CIRCUIT OF MARTON HOLE

I Exit the car park to join the old railway line (The Whitegate Way) going RIGHT, away from the station, to walk to the end of the car park passing toilets and a picnic area to pass a barrier, continue over the final part of the car park and passing another barrier following signs for 'Winsford and Weaver Parkway'. Walk along The Whitegate Way staying RIGHT on the main track at a split and passing by another two path junctions, staying on the main track. After a picnic bench reach a crossroads of paths, with farm buildings ahead on the right.

2 Go RIGHT on the footpath, leaving The Whitegate Way and descending to a

kissing gate. Pass through, going half-RIGHT, over the bottom right-hand corner of a field following a path to pass through another kissing gate into a large field. Go half-LEFT over the next field heading for the left-hand side of two distinct trees as you proceed up the trackless ground. Aim to arrive in the top left-hand corner of the field to reach a gate and kissing gate. Go LEFT through the kissing gate onto the permissive path and 'Walkers Welcome' area to follow track to the top of Marton Hole pool.

3 Here go LEFT, to walk around the pool, keeping it to the right, and continuing to a gate in a hedge, passing through and walking ahead through a plantation towards a fence to reach a track. Go RIGHT, curving right around the pool to reach a gate. The right of way leaves here, so go through the gate on the rightwith the metal gate beside it (staying on the permissive path) and continue, staying right at a path junction to complete a circuit of Marton Hole, curving right again to reach the kissing gate where you began. Go back through it and turn LEFT up the cart track rising towards telegraph posts. At the track end continue ahead up the open field along the right-hand edge. As the field descends, go RIGHT over two stiles to enter a field with a farm ahead. Follow the right of way down the left-hand side of the field to enter the farmyard, and go LEFT before the main yard to cross a stile on the LEFT. Continue over two more stiles and an access track down the left-hand side of buildings to finally exit via a gate in the farmyard.

4 Pass the white house to pick up an access track passing a lake. Cross a cattle grid and curve right to reach a lane at a crossroads. Here go RIGHT to walk past houses on the right and go RIGHT at traffic lights to walk back into the station car park.

A TWO CASTLES TRAIL

DESCRIPTION Prominent from a lot of areas of the Cheshire Plain, and indeed from some areas of North Wales as well, are the two castles of Beeston and Peckforton. Of the pair, Beeston is the more dramatic (and by far the older) set as it is on an easily defended rocky upthrust rising from the surrounding flatlands. The Sandstone Trail traverses the area and some of the more popular, and arguably the best, sections of it pass this way. The route described covers about 5 miles and uses tracks, field paths and a little lane walking to pass through woodland, over the sandstone ridge and across fields with awesome views of Beeston Castle and its cliffs. Allow 3 hours.

START There are two parking areas at the entrance to Beeston Castle. The main castle parking is pay and display and busy in summer, and a little further along the road is a parking area for The Sandstone Trail with picnic benches – this can be locked out of season. SJ 539590.

DIRECTIONS Beeston Castle sits in a neat box formed by four major roads. Both the A49 and the A41 run roughly north/south in this area and the A534 and the A51 go roughly east/west.

BACKGROUND INFORMATION
See page 19

From either car park head south, keeping the walls of Beeston Castle on the right and accessing The Sandstone Trail beyond an information board and via a gate opening. Take the green track into woodland, descending to leave the castle walls and curving left to follow a fence, finally curving right away from this to descend to a road near buildings, exiting the woods via a gate opening. Go LEFT along the road for a few metres to turn RIGHT up steps and through a kissing gate, following The Sandstone Trail over the middle of the field and descending to pass through a kissing gate and carrying on to go half-LEFT over a bridge, staying RIGHT on The Sandstone Trail as the track splits. Climb up steps crossing the next field on the right-hand side to reach a crossing of paths.

Go half-RIGHT following The Sandstone Trail and pass through a kissing gate going half-LEFT over the field to exit via a kissing gate to a crossroads of paths. Go LEFT, then LEFT again following a sign for 'Stonehouse Lane' and walk down the lane to reach a road.

2 Cross the road to go left and then fight on a public footpath as the road bends left. Walk down the field edge. Cross a stile in the fence left further up the field then go right to cross a stile in the field corner and enter the woods. Continue ahead right of a pond. Curve right staying near the edge of the woods. After a pond left cut right through the woods ignoring a stile left. Exit the woods via a stile. Cross the trackless field heading for a kissing gate in the distance. At the kissing gate go right staying on the right side of the fence. Near the field end cut right from the fence to exit the field through a kissing gate in the corner and reach a road. Go right to reach the arched entrance to Peckforton Castle Hotel.

3 Pass under the arch continuing on the access lane to leave it LEFT following yellow arrows just before a '15 mph' sign. Go LEFT uphill to curve right and follow the good track all the way up to pass through a fence and reach a track. Turn RIGHT along it, staying LEFT when it splits almost immediately, and continue to climb up to cross the Peckforton Ridge, well to the left of the Castle. This section is heavily wooded but the paths are good. Continue, to reach a track near a gate on the right and here go LEFT, then turn RIGHT in front of the next gate, following yellow arrows. Descend steps and go down through woods to a hollow and follow the path along it to descend to join The Sandstone Trail at a path junction.

4 Go RIGHT on The Sandstone Trail following the good path through woodland with the Peckforton Ridge to the right and stay on this track until it descends to pass through a kissing gate to join a lane. Here you go RIGHT, walking past houses to reach your outbound route at a path junction. Leave it immediately, going LEFT, following the yellow arrow and

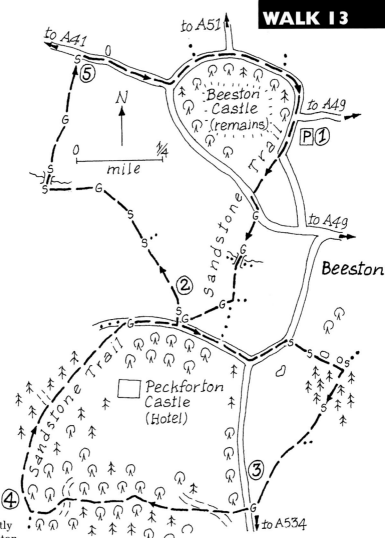

to A51
to A41
to A49
Beeston Castle (remains)
P①
to A49
Beeston
N
mile
Sandstone Trail
Peckforton Castle (Hotel)
Sandstone Trail
to A534
②③④⑤

walking directly towards Beeston Castle. Cross a stile by a gate, descending to join another track at a path junction with a stile ahead. Go over the stile crossing the field on a faint path to cross a second stile. Go half-LEFT in the next field keeping to the lower left part of it, to curve and pass through a gate in the bottom left of the field. Follow the yellow arrow and pick up a cart track and curve right around the right-hand edge of the field next to a hedge. Go RIGHT on the Public Footpath just before a copse, to cross a bridge via two stiles and walk up the right-hand edge of the next field, passing through a kissing gate half way up and carrying on to carefully step over a low electric fence and exit onto a road by Lower Rock Farm via a stile.

5 Go RIGHT along the road towards Beeston Castle cliffs, going LEFT as the road bears right to pick up a lane. Follow this lane keeping the castle walls to the right. Walk around the base of the castle with the ruins and the cliffs to the right. Ignore two left turnings and keep by the wall to arrive back at the parking areas at the entrance to Beeston Castle.

BULKELEY HILL

DESCRIPTION If Bulkeley Hill wasn't covered in trees it would be one of the most distinctive in West Cheshire, with a real pointy, mountain, shape from certain viewpoints. The tree cover, both deciduous and coniferous, does little to detract from this lovely top. In fact, it gives it a lot of character. The Sandstone Trail follows the edge of the hillside high up and this route uses it to work its magical way past sandstone outcrops, where tree-clearing has opened up superb views to the nearby Peckforton Hill and across the Cheshire Plain. Do take care with children on this hillside section, as some of the drops are quite big. This is a short walk of just under 2½ miles and can be done in as little as 1½ hours, but do take longer so you can linger at the viewpoints. The route follows good woodland tracks and paths and includes only a very small section of lane walking to return to your car.

START Parking area at the end of Coppermines Lane near Gallantry Bank. SJ 520550.

DIRECTIONS Coppermines Lane is a minor road leaving the A534 at Gallantry Bank between Broxton and Bulkeley. There is plenty of parking at the lane end. This section of the A534 runs west/east between the A41 and the A49 to the south of Chester and the north of Whitchurch.

BACKGROUND INFORMATION
See page 19

I Walk to the end of Coppermines Lane. Go RIGHT near The Sandstone Trail marker board at the lane end and follow The Trail on a good path directly over the field towards the trees of Bulkeley Hill ahead. Cross a farm track and enter the woods via a kissing gate next to an iron gate. Go half-LEFT, climbing into the woodland on a vague path through trees with an odd marker arrow to guide you. Aim for the right-hand side of a building in the trees above. The path becomes good as you reach a Sandstone Trail marker post to the right of the building and fence. From here follow the path (now

excellent) along the edge of the hillside, keeping the drop to the right. Pass through a fence opening to reach the National Trust sign for Bulkeley Wood and carry on along the edge climbing gradually to curve left to arrive at an information board.

2 From the sign veer left and continue on The Sandstone Trail to curve right and follow the narrowing track down through the trees. At the bottom of some steps, where the track splits, go LEFT heading down towards a gate and cart track to reach a Sandstone Trail Marker post. Join the cart track.

3 Go RIGHT along the track to reach an arch and a gatehouse at a path junction. Here go RIGHT signposted 'Stonehouse Lane'. Descend steeply on a wide sandy path through the trees. Ignore the first turning into the woods on the right and continue until the track begins to level off and the ground on the left opens up, to reach a gate on the right. Here go RIGHT, passing the gate, to enter National Trust land again. Walk forward a few paces to pick up a path and follow it into the trees. Continue and, when a path comes in from the left near old storage tanks, go straight ahead. Join a fence and continue alongside it on the right-hand side to curve right through the woods and cross a distinct surfaced track. Carry on ahead, heading for a white house, to walk to a kissing gate near a road.

4 Don't go through the kissing gate but instead go RIGHT on a footpath and walk uphill beside a wooden fence. When this fence ends carry on ahead, with a wire fence to the left, climbing all the time. When the fence bends sharp right follow the path ahead, climbing much more steeply uphill now to pass sandstone outcrops, and continue to more level ground to reach a kissing gate on the left at the forest edge.

5 Go LEFT through the kissing gate on a path across a field, following yellow arrows. Curve left to descend gradually through trees and continue around the hillside passing markers. Stay on the good path ignoring any turnings off to join a cart

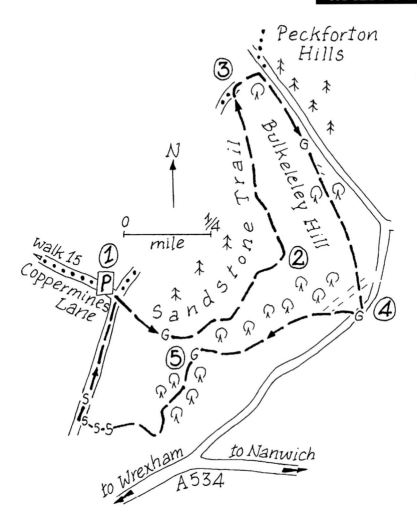

Peckforton Hills

Bulkeleley Hill

Sandstone Trail

N

0   ¼   mile

Walk 15

Coppermines Lane

to Wrexham   *to Nanwich*

A534

track at a junction on a bend. Here you go ahead down the tree-hung track to reach a gate and a stile. Cross the stile to reach a lane by a house. Go to the right of the house to follow the access lane and continue to reach a stile on the right. Cross this, following the path until it peters out. Now head across the bottom left-hand corner of the field diagonally under telegraph wires to reach a stile to the left of a telegraph pole and near a large gorse bush. Cross this to join a lane. Go RIGHT along it for a short distance back to your car.

RAW HEAD & BICKERTON HILL

DESCRIPTION The sandstone ridge that rises above the West Cheshire Plain is great walking country with wooded heights that have sudden and dramatic viewpoints. The Sandstone Trail follows the ridge line and the tree-dotted hillsides, and excellent paths make this a delightful area for an outing. This route does an energetic circuit of Bickerton Hill and Raw Head, which is the highest in west Cheshire at 227 metres.

START Parking area at the end of Coppermines Lane near Gallantry Bank. SJ 520550.

DIRECTIONS Coppermines Lane is a minor road leaving the A534 at Gallantry Bank between Broxton and Bulkeley. There is plenty of parking at the lane end. This section of the A534 runs west/east between the A41 and the A49 to the south of Chester and the north of Whitchurch.

BACKGROUND INFORMATION See page 19

I Walk to the end of Coppermines Lane. Go LEFT near the Sandstone Trail marker board at the lane end and go up the rough lane past 'The Bungalow' on the right. When the lane ends, take the narrower track ahead (The Sandstone Trail) and after a short distance Go LEFT through A kissing gate to take a rising track into woodland. Climb uphill ignoring any turnings off the ridge to the RIGHT. After a good viewpoint on the RIGHT continue to a dip with a yellow arrow marker and an old metal fence on the RIGHT.

2 Take the footpath RIGHT steeply downhill into the trees descending to reach a lane. Go LEFT for about 200 metres and then go RIGHT at a path crossroads to descend through a new plantation. Cross a track, go over a stile and head over the field towards a marker post passing it to reach a stile. Cross the stile and enter the wood and follow the track to finally descend to a stile at the wood edge. Cross this going

immediately LEFT to follow the waymarked path around the left edge of the field around the Mountain Board Centre. Descend through a barrier near a notice board to continue up the track/lane to the road at Hartshill. Go over the road and RIGHT to go LEFT at a cream house. Keep LEFT of the church to pick up a track by the woods LEFT. Keep Park Wood LEFT and pass through two gates with stiles to continue ahead as track bends RIGHT. Cross a stile by a gate following the wood edge LEFT to go LEFT of an electric fence and cross as stile. Continue after the electric fence ends to cross a stile after a gate to descend a field to a further stile before bush line LEFT. Go over and then half-RIGHT to cross three stiles and a bridge and rise up to a road (The A534) via a kissing gate.

3 Go LEFT along the road and then RIGHT up a lane (Smithy Lane) signposted 'Brown Knowle'. Follow this lane through the village eventually passing the Methodist Church on the RIGHT. Take a lane LEFT (Lower Sandy Lane) as the road bends RIGHT. Go RIGHT when the lane splits at the end and the LEFT at a 'T' junction near a house. Stay RIGHT and pass through a gate when the track splits and then go LEFT when it splits again to finally reach a RIGHT bend by wooden bollards and a 'Bickerton Hill' sign. Go ahead through a passing through the bollards and a gate ahead, rise to a fingerpost and then go LEFT leaving the bridleway and following a path towards the hillside. At a path split go ahead (National Trust Arrow) and at the next fork go LEFT and downhill (National Trust Arrow) to reach a crossroads and pick up The Sandstone Trail (straight ahead) signposted 'Maiden Castle'. Climb up to the ridge of Bickerton Hill and go LEFT at a marker post to follow the ridge path over the hill and descend to a col via steps. Stay on The Sandstone Trail, go straight ahead and climb up a gully to go LEFT at the top and walk out to 'Kittys Memorial Stone'.

4 Follow The Sandstone Trail to descend Bickerton Hill and finally reach a road via two kissing gates and a house access road. Go LEFT and over a crossroads by the church to follow the road uphill to cross a major

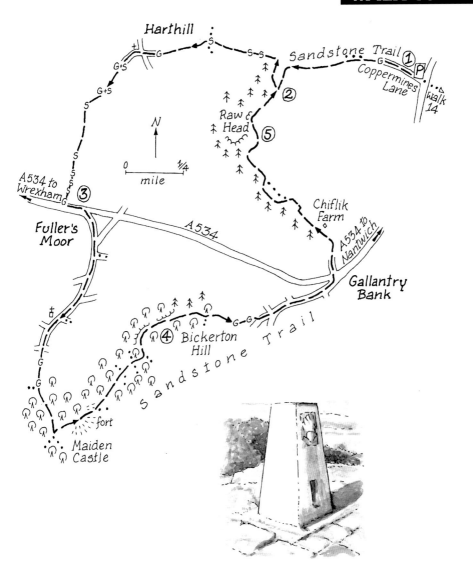

road, going slightly left and up the rough lane on The Sandstone Trail. Climb to Chiflik Farm, pass it on the LEFT and take a grass track uphill. Stay on The Sandstone Trail to climb through the trees, and alongside a wooded ravine LEFT to climb sandstone steps and pass an information board on the LEFT and finally arrive at the trig point on Raw Head summit.

5 Go RIGHT to follow the ridge path to dip to where you left the ridge on your outbound route. Follow the outbound route to descend the hillside, reach a kissing gate and go RIGHT up the rough lane to finally turn RIGHT back into Coppermines Lane and your car.

MARBURY BIG MERE CIRCULAR

DESCRIPTION The southern end of the great sandstone ridge that runs across Cheshire descends finally into lovely and picturesque countryside – a patchwork of meadows and low hillocks. The village of Marbury, with the wonderful St Michael's Church and the Big Mere, is representative of the quality of walking to be found in this area. It is set to the east of the sandstone ridge, and the 3½ mile circuit described below is one of the best in the area. A combination of mereside paths, general footpaths over meadows and fields and some lovely lanes with great views to the sandstone ridge, all link together to give a memorable walk which will take no more than 2½ hours.

START There is roadside parking for a few cars a little outside the village of Marbury on Wrenbury Road, east of the village. Wrenbury Road has the Swan Inn on one side and Little Mere on the other on the outskirts of the village. Please park considerately. SO 454954.

DIRECTIONS Marbury is best found by using Whitchurch (in Shropshire) as a starting point and tracing the two parallel road courses of the A530 (to Nantwich) and the A49 (to Tiverton and Tarporley) northwards. Marbury is located slightly off-centre about between the two, about a third of the way towards Nantwich. It is reached by minor roads. There is little parking in the village itself, so please keep to that indicated above.

BACKGROUND INFORMATION
See page 36

1 Walk up the road in an easterly direction from the parking area to pass a house and reach a crossing of footpaths. Go RIGHT through a kissing gate, and walk down the right-hand side of the field to pass through another kissing gate near a house. Pass by the house on its left-hand side, continuing to reach the access drive. Follow this to exit onto a road via stile and turn RIGHT, heading towards St Michael's Church. Reach a footpath by a gate for the South Cheshire Way. Go LEFT through a gate heading towards the Big Mere on trackless ground to cross a stile in the bottom corner of the field near the Mere, and continue next to the Mere to cross another stile next to a gate. Pick up a rough track running alongside the water and through trees (still on the South Cheshire Way) to reach another stile at the Mere end.

2 Cross the stile, continuing down the next field with a wood on the left. Reach a stile and cross into a field below a house and a gate on the right. Here, leave the South Cheshire Way and go half-RIGHT, following a grassy path and the 'Circular Walk'. Pass below the house and walk up the meadow to reach a gate and stile. Go over the stile and walk half-LEFT up the field, still following the 'Circular Walk', to reach another stile and gate. Go over, continuing up the next field and aiming to the right of the Wicksted Hall ahead. Reach another stile and cross it, passing Wicksted Hall on the right, heading for the prominent mast ahead. Exit onto a lane via a stile.

3 Go RIGHT down the lane, curving right with it as it descends. Stay on the lane past Deemster Manor and carry on along it. It is a fairly quiet lane with excellent views all around. Continue to descend and, as the lane starts to rise up and curve right, go LEFT through a small copse to pick up a footpath. Cross a stile and enter a field. Head half-left up this field, leaving the fence on the left after a short distance to work a way slightly left then curving right and finally left around the bottom of the meadow. Pass under telegraph wires and rise up half-right to reach a stile in the top right-hand corner of the field near a gate. Cross it and drop to a road at a junction.

4 Go directly ahead, ignoring the left turn to walk along the lane. Ignore a footpath turning left towards the canal and continue to reach a gate and footpath sign on the right a little further on.

5 Go RIGHT, taking this footpath which goes half-left over the field, heading

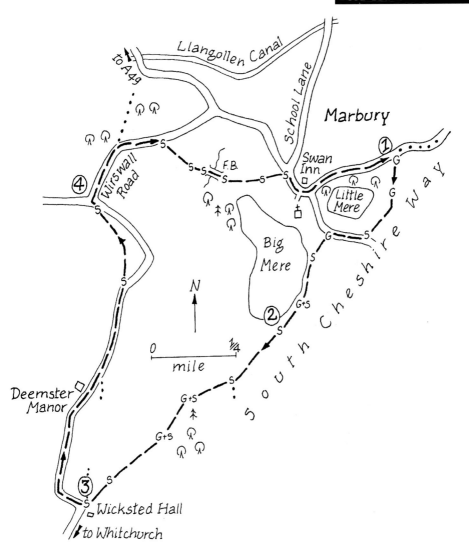

for trees ahead to reach a stile in a hidden corner, about halfway along the field bottom with a drainage ditch to the right of it. Cross the stile descending into the next field and, walking with the brook on the right, cross a bridge via two stiles. Go half-RIGHT to cross another stile then go half-LEFT towards the roof of a building ahead. You reach another stile. Cross this and go half-LEFT, with St Michaels Church across to the right. Go to the left of bungalows to cross a stile near a metal gate and reach a road. Go RIGHT along the road back into Marbury, to go LEFT down Wrenbury road between the Swan Inn and Little Mere to walk through the houses and back to your car.

St. Michaels & All Angels Church, Marbury. Walk 16

WALK 16
MARBURY & THE BIG MERE

WALK 18
BROXTON & CLUTTON

Marbury is a small and typically pretty rural Cheshire village only 4 miles from Whitchurch in Shropshire, and close to the Cheshire/Shropshire border. St Michael's & All Angels Church is very impressive, being set high above Big Mere. It has a long history, and was first mentioned in 1299 although the current building dates from around the 15th century. The pulpit was carved in the 15th century and is believed to be the oldest in Cheshire. There has been some subsidence in recent decades due to the sandy soil of the area.

The churchyard contains the hollow trunk of a one-thousand-year-old yew tree which has been protected by a chain to keep it upright. Local legend has it that if the yew were to topple the church would fall into the mere. Both the Big and Little Mere were formed by receding ice after the last ice age. Big Mere is probably Marbury's greatest claim to fame and is well known to tourists, walkers and cyclists alike. Every year a two-day traditional country fair takes place in the field adjacent to the mere and the church. Usually taking place in the second week of May it has been known to attract over a thousand people.

The South Cheshire Way is a thirty-two mile long distance path linking Grindley Brook to Mow Cop.

Broxton and Clutton are typical of the delightful villages to be found on this western side of the Cheshire sandstone ridge. Both are set on major 'A' roads that provide vital links to the cities and towns of the area. Clutton is passed through on the route but Broxton is only seen from a distance. The most notable resident of Broxton was Harry Atkinson, who went on to become the Premier of New Zealand on four occasions in the late 19th century. This Cheshire village was his birthplace.

36

WALK 19
MALPAS & RESTRICTED BY-WAYS

Malpas is a large border village that in its present day form gives away little of the important role it used to have in the past. Once a regular market town, its name means 'bad passage' from the old French, 'Mal passe'. By-passed now by the busy A41 Chester to Whitchurch road, Malpas used to be a significant staging post on the old Roman road which ran from Shropshire to Chester.

The walk described makes frequent use of 'restricted by-ways' in its later stages and it might be interesting to define just what these are, as a lot of walkers may not know. Basically all roads that were used as public footpaths (surfaced or rough) were re-classified as 'restricted by-ways' in May 2006 when sections 47 – 52 of Countryside and Rights of Way Act (CROW) were implemented. Restricted by-ways and 'roads used as public paths' are not as new as that however, as they were one of the three original categories of public rights of way introduced by the Access to the Countryside Act (1949). However, the term turned out to be confusing and the ways open to misuse by motor vehicles. The CROW Act (originally laid down in 2000) addressed this problem and the re-classified 'restricted by-ways' gave the public the right to pass along them:

- on foot
- on horseback or leading a horse
- by vehicle other than one mechanically propelled (i.e. bike)

In other words you can now walk or ride a horse or bike along them but not drive a car or motorbike along them.

All very legal sounding but, in reality, what they offer walkers are some superb green lanes to walk along and make good time over the land they find themselves upon.

THE RIVER DEE & CHESTER WALLS

DESCRIPTION Chester Tourist Information can be contacted on 01244 402111, and a 'phone call to them a week or so before your visit should give them time to send you information about this fascinating city. The centre of Chester, with the picturesque River Dee flowing by, is well worth taking the time to explore, and the old Roman Walls are impressively intact and give a good circular outing high above the hustle and bustle of the crowds. The route described here takes in a lovely promenade along the banks of the River Dee and you can easily extend this section if you don't mind returning the same way. This route heads back through houses to cross the river on a superb suspension bridge, continues again on the opposite bank and finally climbs onto the walls. From here you simply walk around this ancient city to return to your starting point. The route is just under 3½ miles, and can be done in about two hours, but take your time and leave the walls if you want to explore any part of the city.

START From the Little Roodee car park near Chester Race course. SJ 404656. This is pay and display with a small café on it.

DIRECTIONS Aim to get in the vicinity of the Race Course and the Crown Courts. The Little Roodee car park is opposite the Race Course and below the castle (which is next to the Courts) and you will find the parking area next to the River Dee.

1 Leave the car park by walking with the River Dee to your right and the castle and walls to the left to exit at the bottom of the parking area and follow the paved promenade area along the riverside road. Reach the road end at a road bridge with traffic lights. Carefully cross over and go RIGHT over the bridge, then go LEFT down steps, passing benches. Keep the river on your left and walk along to pass the weir and continue alongside the river, to pass under Queens Park Suspension Bridge and carry on. Reach gates and pass through a kissing

gate to exit into open ground on a riverside trail in a grassy meadow. A good path curves around with the river, with impressive houses over on the opposite bank. Reach a path junction after passing a lifebelt, with a church to the left.

2 Go RIGHT towards houses, heading over heath land. Follow the track to rise to gates by houses. Pass through a kissing gate and walk to a road at a bend. Join Lower Park Road going straight ahead and down it, continuing ahead when Lower Park Road becomes Victoria Crescent. When Victoria Crescent goes left, go RIGHT down a short road to cross Queens Park Suspension Bridge over the River Dee, turning back left towards the river once over. Walk along it and pass the bandstand. Continue with the river on the left and the road on the right until just before the weir to reach sandstone steps on the right rising up onto the city walls.

3 Go up these steps, going RIGHT at the top following the sign for 'Eastgate'. Follow the wall to cross a road via steps and a bridge to continue to reach the clock at Eastgate, overlooking one of Chester's busiest shopping areas. *Note that this area has suffered from long-term repair work – if this is still taking place follow the marked diversion to reach Eastgate Clock.* From Eastgate clock drop down steps and continue along the walls in the direction of King Charles Tower, passing the Cathedral. Pass Abbey Square to reach King Charles Tower.

4 Go sharp LEFT, following the walls with the canal below and to the right. Cross a bridge and descend to cross a modern road bridge at Martins Gate, after Morgan's Mount. After this bridge follow the signs for Water Tower. Descend to reach it.

5 Go sharp LEFT along the walls, crossing a bridge to descend to join a road. Rise up following signs for 'Watergate' to cross the bridge and continue ahead with the Chester Race Course to the right. Continue to a road junction near traffic lights with the castle ahead. Cross carefully and turn RIGHT to cross another smaller road and descend steps to enter the car park near the café.

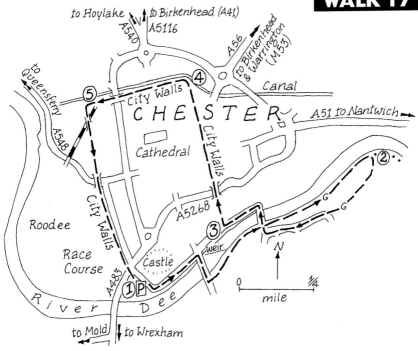

THE RIVER DEE & CHESTER WALLS

Chester is a superb city to visit. As well as typical big city shops there are lots of pretty tourist areas. But it is the City Walls that are the big attraction for many visitors. Basically they are a largely intact defensive system that surround what was the original core of the city. Although many who walk them believe them to be Roman in origin, what you see today is mainly medieval, with some sections Victorian. The original walls were built by the Romans but were constructed of wood and earth around AD 79. These fell into disrepair around 907. Chester Castle was built in 1070 and the walls were given a face lift at this time, and extended.

Chester Walls form an almost complete circular walk of two miles, and are the most complete wall system in the UK. Being elevated above the city, the walk gives you a bird's eye view of both old and new Chester and provides an impressive outing.

The River Dee once brought ships from the sea to the city walls, and has lots of potential for walking.

Part of this walk follows this 70-mile long river, which rises in the Snowdonia National Park and finally discharges into the sea between Wales and the Wirral Peninsula. The weir passed on this route near the Old Dee Bridge was built by Hugh Lupus to supply power to the corn mills.

There is a fish pass on the weir and a fish counting station to monitor the number of salmon ascending the river. Watch for cormorants and herons fishing for eels around this area. An occasional seal has been known to get this far up river on a spring tide.

The Dee Way is a 142-mile long-distance route from the source of the River Dee to the sea, and passes through Chester. A complete guide to this new route is available at www.kittiwake-books.com

ROUND HILL & KING JAMES HILL

DESCRIPTION Round Hill, King James Hill and the area around the lovely Cheshire villages of Broxton and Clutton to the south of Chester constitute the final western foothills of the Sandstone Ridge. This walk is a 6½ mile circuit around this enchanting countryside and is fairly energetic. Some fields can be heavily cropped in the summer season – so please keep to the edges. Allow 3–3½ hours.

START Small roadside parking area with space for two or three cars on the minor lane running south from Clutton to Higher Carden. SJ 466539.

DIRECTIONS From the A41 Chester to Whitchurch road go west from the roundabout on the A534 towards Wrexham. Just before the main part of Clutton village turn left for a little under half a mile. The parking area will be found on the right.

BACKGROUND INFORMATION See page 36

1 Cross the stile at the southern end of the parking area and take the little green track into the woods to cross a further stile, shortly to enter the golf course *KEEPING STRICTLY TO THE RIGHTS OF WAY*. Keep to the right-hand side, with the trees on the right, to cross a track and continue on a good green track. On reaching a path junction continue ahead on the surfaced track and carry on to join the driveway at the clubhouse. Head down it passing the clubhouse on the right. Continue to pass a vineyard and, when the drive bends sharp right near gates ahead, carry straight on, leaving the drive to pass through the gates to pick up the rough track beyond. Descend this to join a lane at a road junction, going LEFT along it to climb up and pass under a bridge. Curve left with the lane heading for the southern end of Round Hill. At a road junction stay LEFT on the lane to curve left. As the lane bends sharp left you reach the end of two driveways. Take the footpath on the RIGHT to climb through a copse, cross a stile and enter a field.

2 Go half-LEFT over the field walking to the left of a small copse and a white house. Cross a stile in the right-hand field corner and head down the right-hand side of the next field to reach a stile in a field corner by a pond. Cross this stile and walk a short way to cross another stile by an oak tree. Cross over a lane and another stile by a gate to enter a field. Cross this field to go over another stile after a rough track and follow the direction of the arrow to cross the next field and pass through a kissing gate. Cross the next field going to the right of a small pond, to pass through a kissing gate to walk across a bridge over a disused railway line. Cross a stile to the left of a gate and enter the next field following the left-hand side of it, going left of a muddy area and keeping to the left of the field to cross a stile in the bottom left-hand corner. Walk a short distance to cross another stile and exit the field to reach the A41 road.

3 Cross over carefully to go LEFT along the road for a short distance and then RIGHT to enter a field via two stiles. Cross the field, going half-LEFT to cross a stile in the right-hand corner of the field, close to where a hedge comes down from the next field. Walk half-LEFT up the next field towards the wooded King James Hill. Go right of a sandy bank to climb steeply to reach a stile halfway along the fence line above. Cross this and go LEFT downhill on the woodland edge to descend to a stile on the left. Cross this and go RIGHT along the field edge with woods to the right. Rise to cross a stile beyond an electric fence. Cross the next field, going RIGHT and staying near the woods. Climb steeply to cross a stile near two tall posts and a gate. Climb to cross another stile and enter woodland. Go LEFT along a green track between fences keeping ahead at a path junction to cross the brow of King James Hill. Curve left just before farm buildings and take the footpath on the LEFT over a stile, to head down the right-hand side of next field, crossing a stile on the right half way down it, after gate. Head down the left-hand side of the next field to cross a stile in the left-hand corner, and follow yellow arrow to cross the next field staying high above the meadow and heading downhill to cross a stile in a left-hand corner of the field as you descend. Head into the meadow below, then climb out of it to pass through a kissing gate and reach the A534 road.

4 Cross the road carefully, to walk along Withy Lane on the other side and continuing along it until shortly before a road junction, where you take the footpath on the left down the side of a fence to enter a large field. NOTE – *in very wet weather or if in crop it may be best to continue ahead on the lane and stay left to join the A41 and walk back (carefully) down it to reach point 5*. Head down the field going to the left of a copse. Continue to go right of the next copse, turning RIGHT as you reach it to arrive at the bottom of the field near the

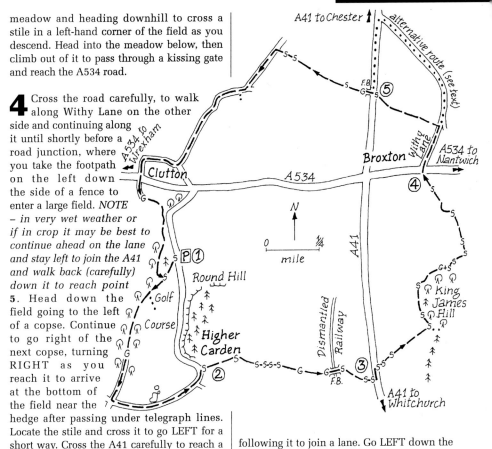

hedge after passing under telegraph lines. Locate the stile and cross it to go LEFT for a short way. Cross the A41 carefully to reach a footpath.

5 Go RIGHT to cross a little bridge following the right of way and passing though a gate. Follow the green track to cross a stile to enter a field. Go down the right-hand edge of it, keeping to the left of the farm yard and passing through a farm storage area. The path is very vague but crosses the field ahead half-RIGHT, heading for the buildings ahead. Again if the field is in crop walk around the edge of it on the right, keeping to the rough bits. Either way the destination is a little to the left of the bottom right-hand corner of the field where you will find a stile in the fence. Cross the stile and walk to cross a driveway and reach another stile to the right of a brick building. Cross this to go half-RIGHT and walk down the track to the right of the house and join a surfaced road,

following it to join a lane. Go LEFT down the lane and walk back to Clutton. Stay RIGHT at a junction near houses to enter the village and finally curve sharp left to walk up to the A534 near a road sign for 'Nantwich'. Cross carefully, taking the footpath up a track. Curve left between hedges to reach houses at Garden Smithy. Here curve left to pass to the left of a gate and enter woodland. Follow the track into more open country to bend right and pass through a fence gap. Climb uphill into trees again. Climb steadily to pass though a fence gap and re-enter the golf course. Follow the fenced track through it to go LEFT at a sign and then RIGHT by signs to drop down through trees on a good path. You reach a path junction and your outbound route. Here go LEFT along the golf course edge to reach a stile in the left-hand corner of the field. Cross this and walk back down the track and over the next stile to your car.

MALPAS & OVERTON SCAR

DESCRIPTION Malpas is a great centre for a walk on the edge of west Cheshire hill country. Extensive use is made of 'restricted by-ways' on this circular route, which is just slightly under 6 miles. The long distance horse-trekking route of Bishop Bennet Way is also followed and the extensive local network of field paths is put to good use. There are great views over the border into Wales, and the Clwydian range looks close and inviting. Overton Scar is a wonderful ridge of elevated sandstone and the only real shame is that there is no right of way along the crest of it – this walk follows the wooded base underneath the crags. Odd gates give access to the top but officially you should not be there. This is a delightful outing and if you do it in a morning you could follow it with lunch in the quaint village centre of Malpas afterwards. Allow 3 hours.

START There are two free car parks in Malpas village centre, and this walk can be started from either. We have chosen to use the one adjacent to the village Fire Station (The Cheshire Fire Brigade Malpas Training Ground) which is open 08.00 – 18.00 daily. SJ 487474.

DIRECTIONS If you use the A41 Chester to Whitchurch road you will not go far wrong. Malpas is located slightly north of Whitchurch and west of the A41 on the junction of the B5395 and the B5069. If you approach from the A41 on the B5395 heading south west, the fire station and car park will be found on your left, shortly after you enter the village but before you reach the shops.

BACKGROUND INFORMATION
See page 37

I Walk to the bottom right of the car park away from the Fire Station to exit via a gate following signs for 'The Village'. Go RIGHT on a track, with houses to the left, and walk along this to join a road going left past a bus stop. Reach 'High Street' at a junction and go LEFT crossing over the road when safe to do so. At the stone memorial

go RIGHT up Church Street to pass by St Oswald's Parish Church. It is worth taking a detour into the churchyard for a quick look around this lovely building. Having passed the church go RIGHT, following the public footpath down a track to turn LEFT just before the Rectory, following signs for 'The Marches Way'. Go through an opening to go to the right of a building, curving left past it and walking down the drive to reach a gate. Pass through into open country and a path junction. Take the path ahead directly over the field, heading towards playing fields, to pass through a kissing gate and enter football fields. The next kissing gate is roughly behind the far goal area of the right-hand pitch, so go around it to the right to pass through this. Walk ahead to pass through two kissing gates to enter a field. Go half-RIGHT over the field (*if the field is in crop go around the edge – this applies to all the fields on the early part of this route*) to reach and pass through a kissing gate, pass through to go half-LEFT over the centre of the next field heading towards gates in the left-hand corner and gradually descending. Pass through the kissing gate going diagonally half RIGHT over the next field. Pass through a kissing gate halfway along the field bottom. Cross an overgrown track and pass through another kissing gate into a field. Walk down left-hand edge of this field and pass through the kissing gate in the bottom left-hand corner to walk down the right-hand side of the next field to reach a green lane via a stile in the right-hand corner of the field. This is Bishop Bennet Way.

2 Go RIGHT up the track, pass through a gate and carry on along the wide track to curve gently right and reach a lane. Go LEFT along the lane, passing Overton Heath. After Corner Cottage, when the road goes sharp right, leave it, going ahead on a green track following Bishop Bennet Way. Follow this to reach gates, pass through and continue, to pass through three gates (or openings) and passing farm buildings. Shortly after the farmyard, begin to climb up passing odd sandstone outcrops. Stay on the track to curve right under Overton Scar to reach a path junction as Bishop Bennet Way goes sharp left.

reach Overton Heath Lane at a corner and go LEFT along it to reach a T-junction facing a house.

5 Go LEFT for a few yards, then go RIGHT through an opening after the house, to pick up the footpath on a track over the field. Continue to pass into the next field via a stile and descend gradually, passing a pond on the left and following yellow arrows to re-enter the field. Continue down the right-hand side of it. Reach a stile in the right-hand corner and cross it to go over a bridge and enter the next field. Continue along the rough track to follow the right-hand edge of the field, dropping down just before the field narrows, to reach a stile in a sunken area. Cross the stile and head down a green track between fences. Turn RIGHT near the end and walk forward a few paces to reach a track (another 'restricted by-way') with a lane on the left. Go RIGHT uphill, climbing steadily to reach a more level area while ignoring any turnings off. Follow the good track to pass a school and reach houses via a gate at the track end. This is Hollow Wood. Go ahead on the road to walk downhill through the houses to reach the main road. Go RIGHT along it, crossing over when it is safe. Walk back into Malpas watching for the LEFT turn back to the car park, just before the village centre.

3 Leave the track to go ahead and cross a stile to follow the right-hand edge of the field under Overton Scar, curving RIGHT into the bottom right-hand corner to cross a stile by a gate. Continue on a narrow path to cross another stile and enter a field, continuing along the right-hand edge to cross a stile. Go half-LEFT by a fence to curve right and join a drive. Go LEFT down it, walking to a Whitewood Lane and going RIGHT along it. At a road junction go RIGHT (signposted Malpas) climbing up to follow the lane as it levels out. As the lane bends sharp left after a white cottage, reach a track going RIGHT, signposted 'by-way to Malpas'.

4 Take this to go to the right of Gamswood Cottage and climb up through Gams Wood, passing a sandstone outcrop and continue to reach a lane after a red bricked house. Go RIGHT on the bridleway, taking the track to the right of houses. Descend to

43

WALK 20

THE BAKER WAY

DESCRIPTION As most of the walks in this book have used one or another of the long distance paths that criss-cross this area of Cheshire, it seems appropriate that the last route included should follow the course of one of these entertaining outings. We have chosen The Baker Way as it links up the great City of Chester with Delamere Forest, cutting across the West Cheshire Plain with the sandstone ridge ahead and to the right for a lot of the way. It finally ends in the forest at Delamere and gives a great outing of about 13 miles that should take just over 6 hours or so. It is quite a demanding walk following field paths, bridleways, tracks and lanes, and avoids a lot of the busier places of the region by clever routing. This is a linear route, but as it starts at Chester railway station and ends at Delamere railway station, the problems of getting back to your starting point are easily sorted out. Although the route is described from Chester heading east to Delamere and then catching the train back to Chester, it can be done just as easily in the opposite direction. There seems to be a train from Delamere back to Chester around 25 minutes past most hours (Mon-Sat) but check before you set out by

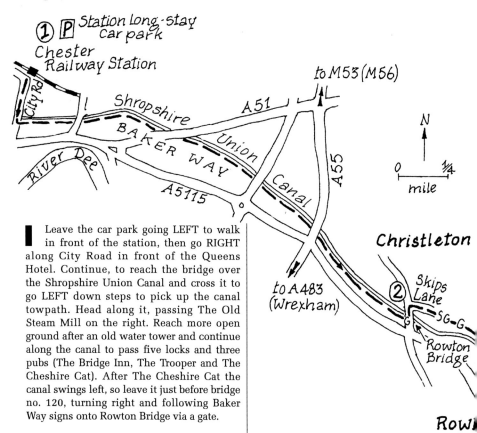

Leave the car park going LEFT to walk in front of the station, then go RIGHT along City Road in front of the Queens Hotel. Continue, to reach the bridge over the Shropshire Union Canal and cross it to go LEFT down steps to pick up the canal towpath. Head along it, passing The Old Steam Mill on the right. Reach more open ground after an old water tower and continue along the canal to pass five locks and three pubs (The Bridge Inn, The Trooper and The Cheshire Cat). After The Cheshire Cat the canal swings left, so leave it just before bridge no. 120, turning right and following Baker Way signs onto Rowton Bridge via a gate.

44

ringing National Rail Enquiries on 0845 7484950 or The Cheshire Travel Line on 01244 602666.

START From the long stay car park at Chester Railway station. SJ 411670. This is pay and display and will cost you £4.50 for the day (2009).

DIRECTIONS Chester is a big city, and the traffic can be heavy, so aim to arrive early to make sure you get a parking place. Once in Chester, no matter how you enter the city, head towards the city centre and watch out for the station signs. Once you pick them up follow them to find the parking area which is to the left of the station.

2 Go LEFT on the lane and walk along it to go RIGHT down Skips Lane. At the end of this take a narrow track going to the left of the last house to walk down a narrow lane and pass through a squeeze stile and later a kissing gate to enter a field. Walk diagonally half-RIGHT across it, passing through another kissing gate and going straight on over the next field to re-join the canal on the opposite bank. Go LEFT along this, passing through a kissing gate and continuing to finally drop half-LEFT off the canal into a copse. Pass through a kissing gate and go down the left of the next field. Cross a stile into another field and go down the left-hand side of it to cross a stile near a field gap. From here walk to a kissing gate and a junction of paths. Go ahead on the green track to reach Brown Heath Road via a kissing gate. Cross straight over to

take a footpath down a drive and at the end of this go to the right of the white house. Take a footpath to the left of a shed and the right of a garage, going down a narrow track to enter a field via a kissing gate. Cross the next field passing in between two ponds and exit via a bridge and kissing gate into a field. Cross over three fields and go through two kissing gates to cross a track and walk up a narrow lane for a short distance to enter a field. Here go half-LEFT towards the smaller of two oak trees to exit to Plough Lane via a kissing gate. Go RIGHT down this and continue ahead when it bends left. This is Platts Lane. Follow it down to continue ahead at Cotton Farm and at the road end carry on down a track to cross an old bridge. Continue over two more bridges crossing the River Gowy. This area is known as Hockenhull Platts. Follow a good track through the woods climbing to reach a path junction. Go LEFT, climbing to exit the track after passing an egg factory. Reach a road junction and continue ahead, following a yellow arrow to walk to reach the busy A51.

route continues on next page →

3 Cross the A51 *very carefully*, passing through a gate on the other side and continuing ahead to pass through another gate by a barrier. Walk through a woodland area to join Hockenhull Lane at Tarvin. At end of the lane go RIGHT (still on Hockenhull Lane) and continue on it until you reach Tarvin High Street at a T-junction. Go RIGHT to walk by the shops, keeping LEFT at the George and Dragon pub to walk out of the town and reach the A54. Again, cross the road carefully, to go LEFT once over, signposted 'Tarvin Mill', and immediately branch RIGHT onto Sandy Lane. Follow this to its end at a T-junction. Cross over, going over a stile and following The Baker Way down the field to pass through a gate into a big field. Go directly ahead to reach a stile to the left of trees near the bottom right of the field. Cross it to reach the bridge over Salters Brook.

4 Cross this and go over the next field, going to the right of the hedge and trees and following the left-hand side of it along to reach a drive. Here go LEFT and then RIGHT to go to the left of the hedge and walk up the field. Continue to a gap crossing a stream on a raised area and go half-RIGHT over the next field to exit into the next field via a kissing gate. Go directly over it and cross a stile to reach a narrow green track. Go LEFT up it and, when it ends, cross a stile to head to the bottom left-hand corner to cross a bridge

and go RIGHT along the right-hand edge of the sloping field, to exit via a stile onto a farm lane. Go LEFT uphill to reach Peel Hall Farm. Curve left into the farmyard and, just before buildings, go RIGHT down a narrow lane behind a barn. At the end of this lane go LEFT through a gate opening to go RIGHT, and walk past barns and by a large wall. Continue through another gate to pass Peel Hall on the left-hand side and curve right in front of the hall, continuing on the good track

with a fence on the left to reach a T-junction by a cream-coloured house. Cross the road and go over the stile to follow the green lane to a gate. Cross a stile and head down the left-hand side of the next field. Cross a stile by a gate and continue to pass through a small kissing gate and follow the right edge of the next field, curving right near the end of it to walk to a stile. Cross it to reach a road. Cross over to go LEFT on the permissive path. Descend to cross a drive entrance, continuing on the road to pass to the right of a bench and pick up Grange Lane. Follow this to pass Ashton Grange and descend to pass fishing ponds and climb up again to pass a house, continuing on to go RIGHT at the lane T-junction. Just before Woodside Farm go LEFT down a footpath to reach a road. Cross over, pass a barrier and enter woodland and go immediately LEFT to descend on a path to a picnic area and a car park at Brine's Brow.

Mouldsw
fishing ponds
Lar
Grange
The Gran
Peel Hall
Ashton Hayes

N

0 — ¼ mile

Salter Brook
Sandy Lane
Tarvin Mill
A54
A54
High St
CROSS WITH CARE!
Tarvin
CROSS WITH CARE!
A51
Hockenhull Lane

continued from previous page

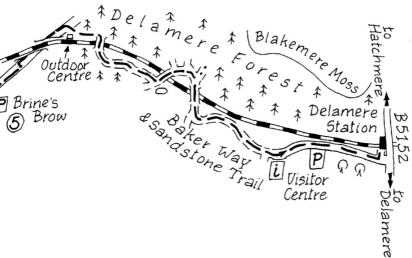

5 Exit the car park, going RIGHT along the road to cross over before a railway bridge, and pass under it on the left-hand side of road. Continue ahead into the forest, passing an outdoor centre, and follow the road for about two hundred metres to go RIGHT on The Baker Way near a barrier. Walk uphill into trees to climb to a railway line turning LEFT to walk along to a railway bridge. Go LEFT over it then go straight ahead into the woods. Curve left and go LEFT at the T-junction to re-cross the railway. (The Baker Way is well marked through the forest). Continue ahead at the next junction and curve right to join the Sandstone Trail at a T-junction. Go RIGHT on the Baker Way and Sandstone Trail to cross the railway via a bridge for the third time. Go ahead at the next junction, climbing slightly uphill to a path junction near a fence. Here go LEFT and descend to cross a brook, climbing back up to follow the path and, when the track bears left, to go over a railway bridge. Go RIGHT just after a bench and head downhill to climb up again. Follow the track all the way to reach a lane. Here go LEFT and walk to the Forest Visitor Centre. Pass it and cross the railway bridge ahead. Shortly after it turn LEFT on a track towards the railway line and go through woods to walk to a car park. Walk through this to reach Delamere Railway Station at the end of The Baker Way.

THE BAKER WAY

This is a great walk and a nice way to link Chester to the Delamere Forest. The original Baker Way (of which the current route is an extended and re-worked version) was devised by members of the Mid Cheshire Footpaths Association to commemorate the life and work of one Jack Baker, a one time Footpath Officer for Cheshire County Council.

The walk can be muddy after rain and although thirteen miles may not sound far, make sure you are up to it. A lot of regular walkers do 7 or 8 mile routes at weekends, but to suddenly double the distance can be daunting. Despite crossing well-inhabited areas The Way does its best to avoid civilisation and has a real feeling of remoteness about it. Waymarking is generally good, with yellow arrows bearing the 'Baker Way' logo, but the route described above (west to east) has one or two under-marked areas – the area from Peel Hall to Brines Brow in particular being a little vague.

KEY TO THE MAPS

- → Walk route and direction
- === Metalled road
- ‒‒‒ Unsurfaced road
- .... Footpath/route adjoining walk route
- ~~→ River/stream
- 木 ↷ Trees
- ■□■ Railway
- **G** Gate
- **S** Stile
- ⩘ Viewpoint
- P Parking
- T Telephone

THE COUNTRY CODE

- Be safe – plan ahead and follow any signs

- Leave gates and property as you find them

- Protect plants and animals, and take your litter home

- Keep dogs under close control

- Consider other people

About the author, Steve Goodier...

Steve is a life-long outdoor enthusiast who has walked and climbed all over the United Kingdom and in many other parts of the world. He is a freelance writer based in Cheshire who produces regular routes for the likes of Country Walking Magazine as well as Walking Wales and Cumbria Magazine. A family man with two growing children, he spends as much of his spare time as he can camping and walking in our National Parks and mountain regions with the Lake District and Scotland being his personal favourites.

Published by
Kittiwake Books Limited
3 Glantwymyn Village Workshops,
Glantwymyn, Machynlleth, Montgomeryshire
SY20 8LY

© Text & map research: Steve Goodier 2010
© Maps (from ooc base): Kittiwake 2010
© Illustrations: Morag Perrott 2010

Cover photographs: *Main:* Raw Head.
Inset: Marbury Mere. Steve Goodier.

Care has been taken to be accurate. However neither the author nor the publisher can accept responsibility for any errors which may appear, or their consequences. If you are in doubt about any access, check before you proceed.

Revisions 2013.

Printed Mixam, UK.

ISBN: 978 1 902302 74 4